# TOO HAPPY TO BE
## Sad Girl

### SURVIVING SADNESS, DITCHING ANXIETY
### AND LEARNING TO THRIVE

## ANGEL AVILES

DISCLAIMER: THIS BOOK DOES NOT PROVIDE MEDICAL ADVICE.

The contents of this book are solely for general informational and educational purposes, and are not intended or implied to provide medical or other professional health care advice, nor are they intended to be used to assess health conditions or to be substituted for professional medical advice. Always seek the advice of your physician or other qualified health care professional relating to any concerns you may have regarding symptoms, of depression, panic or anxiety disorder.

To request permissions, contact the publisher at angel@toohappytobesadgirl.com

ISBN: 9798650442738 (Paperback)

ISBN: 9781393374312(Ebook)

First paperback edition November 2020.

Library of Congress Control Number: 2020911472

Printed in the USA.
Angel Aviles
2355 Westwood Blvd #339
Los Angeles, Ca. 90064

TooHappyToBeSadgirl.com

# Contents

# The Truth y Que

BEGINNINGS CAN BE complicated, so I'm going to start in the middle if that's okay with you.

I facilitate wellness training workshops and coach people through complicated life transitions. I didn't get a formal education for this type of work. However, I came upon this career path in the most authentic way: I lived and grew through intimate experiences with death, addiction, divorce, fear, anxiety, panic, and pain.

Then I just got bold enough to talk about it openly.

I grew brave enough to publicly share my process of soulful restoration. And people listened. At first I was shocked at how much people listened. On social media, I had a few thousand followers who mostly knew me from my work on the film *Mi Vida Loca*. But then I started getting the emails and messages. People were sharing their darkest moments and thanking me for helping them change their lives. It was humbling, but I understood why they felt they could speak so freely.

Marianne Williamson wrote, "Our deepest fear is not that we are inadequate. Our deepest fear is that we are powerful beyond measure. It is our light, not our darkness that most frightens us."

I was sharing my light and people were inspired.

I'm not a guru. Back in the day, everybody and their mama

were marketing themselves as gurus, which, now that I think of
it, was kind of disrespectful. The original gurus were the spiritual leaders of Hinduism and Buddhism. In the early 2000s,
the term got hijacked. Gurus were popping up all over the
place. Some of these gurus were about as spiritual as a kick in
the ass. Still, they were good marketers, and I gave them props
for that. There were others, however, who called themselves
gurus less than a day after taking a class. This, for some reason,
made me cringe.

At that time, I worked in digital marketing. Myspace was
replaced by Facebook, and a new social network called YouTube
popped up. Industry experts wondered if a streaming video
platform was a waste of time for grown folks, and they scru-
tinized Google's purchase. You have to understand that early
on, there were a lot of cat videos but no sign of influencers or
broadcast channels. Things changed fast, and there was a lot to
keep up with. I studied and forced myself to learn at the speed
of change, and although I knew a lot, I never felt like I knew
enough to label myself a guru.

And THAT was the story of my life. On the surface, no
matter what I did or accomplished, I never felt like I was good
enough. When I dug deeper into my patterns of behavior, I
realized that this persistent insecurity kept me from following
through on certain things. It kept me from acknowledging my
successes. And it was a breeding ground for anxiety.

You opened this book for a reason. Maybe it's just because
you know and love Sad Girl. But I suspect some of you are
familiar with anxiety, and I'm going to gamble that you can
also relate to the chronic feeling of not-enoughness.

I once read a quote that said, "There are people less qualified than you doing the things you want to do simply because
they decided to believe in themselves." These words resonated
in my soul when I read them. This is really why it bothered

me when certain people called themselves gurus! They may not have been experts, but they had the guts to declare their understanding and be confident in their ability to learn. I was jealous. I was insecure.

I'm jumping right into this because if you're struggling with self-worth, being overly critical, and full of fear—I want you to know that you're not alone. It has taken me ten years to write this book. Ten fucking years. It's autobiographical! How much more time could I possibly need to become an expert at living my life?

I've been on television and in movies, and I've worked for some huge companies. I've met thousands of people who are fans—some who stood in line for hours to meet me. But still, my prevailing thoughts of insufficiency lingered.

I've learned that this feeling of inadequacy has a proper name: imposter syndrome. This is a psychological term used to describe people who doubt their accomplishments and have a persistent fear of being exposed as a fraud. Psychologists Pauline Clance and Suzanne Imes coined it in an article written in 1978. Forty years later, this syndrome is still robbing people of the pleasure they deserve to experience. How sad! Today most of us with this syndrome spend countless hours trying to do the best we can at school, at work, as parents, as community members, and more. What we don't know is that no matter how badass we are, most of us are walking around feeling like total fakes.

If you decide to read on and come along for a ride through my life, you'll learn a few of the cultural reasons why this idea—this feeling, this affliction—has plagued me. You'll also find out how and why I continue to work to shake imposter syndrome, not just for myself but for others as well. I owe that to the badasses who came before me and to those who will follow.

By the way, someone else popularized the term *badass*, and

though I love it, I'm going to have to leave it behind in this paragraph. From here on out, in honor of the Chicana influences in my life, I will be using the term *chingona*. Feel free to replace it with *chingonx* if you're non–gender-conforming.

Within these pages you'll find my life experiences mixed in with the techniques and processes that I've used to understand and manage my anxiety. It takes courage to speak the truth and even more to live in it. But this baring of my soul is for my kind. My kind are those of you who never seem to have time to discover your talents because you spend most of your time making sure everyone else is living their best life. You're also my kind if you know your gifts but don't share them with the world because you feel like an imposter! It's a vicious little cycle when we get caught up in the mindset of scarcity or not-enoughness.

As you read on, you'll learn that I've spent time in some pretty dark places. Regardless of where I've been, I now know that if I can bring it back to being okay with the real me, I'm good.

As an influencer, I've had to consider how much of the real me I give and when. In my online presence, I always try to keep it real with a positive twist. For the most part, I can do that by asking myself three questions:

Does this need to be said?

Does this need to be said by me?

Does this need to be said by me right now?

I got these questions from Justin Bariso, an expert on the topic of emotional intelligence. He found this sage advice from watching an interview with a comedian who had been married three times. Sometimes we need to fail to really understand something. How do I know? Because I've learned through failure in more ways than I can count!

As kids so many of us fantasize about being famous, but

it's a challenge to live a public life. There are two situations in which I know I'm setting myself up to feel like a failure:

Number one is when I find myself evaluating whether real-life moments are Instagram- or Pinterest-worthy. My kids will totally check me on this by insisting I not post or that I take only one photo and enjoy the moment. They are one hundred percent correct. As tempting as it is to acquire likes to make myself feel good, it's a trap. I can't live in the moment and also focus on the praise of people in my virtual world.

Number two on the road to feeling like a failure is when I get caught up in shitty comments. The malicious scrutiny of strangers can be overwhelming. And just like I can't get caught up in praise, I also have to avoid getting caught up in destructive criticism. My ego will want to engage, but again, it's a trap.

My mom used to say, "Nadie sabe lo que hay en la olla más que la cuchara que la menea." Which translates to, "No one knows what's in the pot more than the spoon that stirs it." We just don't know what's going on in people's lives and, more importantly, in their heads.

In the age of social media, where everything seems so freakin' perfect, imposter syndrome is at an all-time high. According to one clinical research paper published by the International Journal of Behavioral Science (Vol. 6, No.1, 75-97), an estimated 70 percent of the US population has experienced some form of it. So, right now, no matter how chingona that influencer you admire is, or how amazing the person who's doing what you want to do is, there's a good chance they feel like a phony!

I'm mostly over that now. But even as I write this book, I still have lingering thoughts about all my failures. I've lost jobs, been fired, kissed frogs, failed at businesses, and betrayed relationships. Some days I think, Who am I to encourage anyone? I think about the fantastic books I've read over the years—books filled with tales of women who found their purpose while traveling across Italy, award-winning stories by poetic monks, and the chronicles of heroes who survived horrific injustices.

I have to admit that part of me feels like mine is just a story about an ordinary brown girl from the Bronx; it just doesn't sound like a bestseller. Thankfully, another part of me is like, Fuck it! There are too many of us who've minimized our experiences and dulled our shine. My kind need to know that every journey documented stands to make an impact.

So I'm writing this book. Despite the voices I have to squash, I'm sharing—and I'm not stopping myself. I don't do that to myself anymore. The journey has been long A.F.! Seriously, I'm fifty. If you can get over the kind of dumb shit I've had to get over in half the time I did, God bless you! I want it for you. That's why I'm pouring myself out onto paper.

Imposter syndrome is a perfect diagnosis for people like me. For most of my life, I've floated between boxes of categories that I never really fit into anyway. Some of you know how hard it is to cram yourself into behavioral boxes that aren't yours. Some boxes come from our parents, our peers, or our society, and they're usually designed to keep us safe but rarely tailored to feed our souls. My boxes were set up to keep me feeling like I was either not enough of something or just too much of everything else. Over the years, I've been not: brown enough, white enough, classy enough, hood enough, wealthy enough, or broke enough. I've also been: too emotional, too cold-hearted, too fat, too skinny, too harsh, too silly, too intense, too young, too old.

For me, fitting in just got too exhausting. I had to create the space to be me.

If you've been on the quest to find yourself for a while, you'll know that the internet can be a rabbit hole. Don't get me wrong, I'm online for work and play for many hours of the day. But sometimes information can get overwhelming.

I remember reading at one point a whole lot of posts online with the hashtag #DoYou.

Do you? Such a simple little phrase, but in a world where so many people seem to copy one another, I had to ask myself exactly what it meant to do me. I figured out that doing me meant being as real and in the moment as possible. I also realized that being real and in the moment didn't happen naturally or simultaneously without re-training. Doing me means being willing to risk not being accepted by some and choosing to pursue my happiness. It means learning and growing from the choices I make and not blaming or making excuses for others or myself.

Doing me has come at a price, mostly in the form of internal battles. At fifty I realize that doing me can seem selfish. Doing me has meant doing what makes me happy, peaceful, secure, and prosperous. It can have a direct connection to someone else's sadness or disappointment, and I must live with that. But doing me has NOT resulted in me mercilessly trampling on others. I can set boundaries, look out for my best interest, and not be a bitch.

I can also decide to be a bitch. Hello! That part of me is not dead.

I can choose to serve the needs of others, too. Doing me is about balance. The art of doing me allows me to make choices and trust the consequences.

In these pages I'll share what I've realized about life, love, and the art of doing me in the hopes that you'll be encouraged and inspired to really DO YOU.

So as you surely now know, I'm not a guru. I'm not a doctor or therapist, either. So what am I?

If I were forced at gunpoint to put a label on how I would want you to view me, it would either be as your tía (*aunt*) who is crazy like a fox, or a trusted comadre. I have a bit of both of those characters in me. In my mind, tías are fun and trustworthy, and they enjoy the benefit of being older and wiser but free from the burden of parenting. A tia's advice can somehow be both kind and brutally honest without having the same tone as a mom's advice.

Now, *comadre* means *co-mother*. For many of us, a comadre is your ride-or-die homegirl—someone you would trust with your baby's life. Google says *comadre* means *midwife*. I like that. I'd want to be the person who helps you give birth to the next best version of you.

So yeah, if you see me, you can call me tía or comadre! Some say I'm a teacher, a guide, a friend, and even a light. I'm happy to be all those things, but really these pages are just some words of wisdom from your local neighborhood chingona.

Chingona is not a title I take lightly, and it took a lot of effort to get here.

The idea for this book came up out of a midlife shift in my life. I guess I could call it a crisis if I wanted to sound dramatic. They were some high-pressure years of living and learning. Some of the moments that I've documented are embarrassing; some are fun and full of joy. I'm just going to share what happened to me when I permitted myself to change my way of thinking. Unlike the negative labels society tends to place on midlife, I ultimately came to love that stage. My late thirties were a time of dissolution. Figuring out how to let go of so many things was a hard but necessary part of my journey. My forties were a time of rebirth and transformation.

Frankly, age doesn't matter much at all. If you feel like a giant shift is happening right now and you don't know what to do with yourself, it's okay! Starting now, you get to look at the places you've gone, real or imagined, and make some observations about how you've been living. You get to decide if you want to keep living like that or if you're ready for change.

Growing often comes with pain or discomfort, and we often want to skip that part. We want to slide past fear and push past pain so we don't have to feel it. The truth is that we can make it through all of it—the ups and downs, the entire ride. It's all a part of life. And the real trip is where we find our deepest fears. That's actually where our real magic is.

It's crazy that we run from the dark. We miss out on so much when we run from what pain is trying to teach us. My transformation into the woman I am today took me years. I could lie and say that things were easy, but that would make this the shortest book ever. And you'd be mad when you got to the end. The truth is that the suggestions in this book are simple, but a real transformation isn't comfortable. You may have to make some hard decisions—decisions that change your life and maybe even hurt people's feelings.

Over the years I uncovered some "truths" about myself, only to realize that they were just beliefs. In other words, they were ideas that I'd held on to. These ideas had nothing to do with my purpose in life; they were just concepts I'd picked up and adopted as my own. When I fell into my dark and seemingly endless hole of loneliness and anxiety, I desperately wanted to accept who I had become but I couldn't. Who I had become just didn't match who I felt I was meant to be.

As I slid further down into that cold, forsaken space inside myself, a frantic need grew in me. I wanted to feel good.

When I started my journey into self-discovery, it was like meeting someone new. I found out that I wasn't a fraud, I hadn't totally failed in life, and I wasn't destined to live the rest of my days in misery. I just needed a change. I just needed some time to adjust my course.

Think about what I'm saying to you. I had spent years being sick, depressed, anxious, and flipped out because I wasn't living authentically! Was it a surprise that imposter syndrome kept me nearly paralyzed? Please hear me when I tell you that I wasn't walking around being consciously fake. That's not it at all. I just wasn't fully living my truth, and there's a difference.

Have you ever buried parts of your past so that you could live a new life detached from the experiences that you were afraid or ashamed of? Doing so isn't as much a lie as it is a form of survival. The reality of our experience, regardless of how deep we bury it, eventually comes up like a weed. We can lie to ourselves and others or do whatever it takes to protect our beliefs about the truth. But what is the truth? Every circumstance requiring proof of truth involves observation, and the observer has a lot to do with the facts recorded around the truth. The truth and our convictions can get pretty complicated, mainly because we interchange them so much.

History books have been filled with "facts" that were recorded and accepted as real. Generation upon generation are then taught that these "truths" are something to fashion a belief system around. Somehow, opposing accounts of history emerge and different perspectives are introduced—despite the desire to keep them hidden. Inevitably there's conflict because it's hard for people to accept that an entire belief system is based on opinion or, worse, lies. Sometimes we're unwilling to question some of the ideas we've come to believe as the absolute truth.

This is why I call what's in these pages MY truth. Maybe we'll come to agree on some points, but your truth has to be yours.

This book is about how I discovered that my truth was solid but that I have to check on my beliefs daily. Beliefs are living things. I'm willing to bet that you have believed some pretty unreal shit, even about yourself. My guess is that, at least once you've chosen to accept a lie because it just seemed less complicated than facing the truth. I'm not saying you were a straight-up fool, but getting to the bottom of things isn't always easy.

Some of us have spent most of our lives living up to a fraction of our potential because we've believed in someone else's truth more than we've believed in our own. Some of us know we should do more, have more, and be more but we've been trapped in a mediocre life. Do you feel trapped in mediocrity?

Here's a truth bomb for those of you who answered yes: You're the reason you're trapped.

You won't allow yourself to be bigger than the experiences you've already had. And whatever details lie behind your beliefs about the truth, the bottom line is fear.

What? Yep. Half the people in your life would never know you're afraid because your life may look good on you. I get it! Mine did too. But this book is about growing, and you can't build a big life inside a small mind.

Most of us are, in fact, small-minded. I hate to say that, but it's true. And it's okay. The small mind is a cozy place. We want to fit in, be safe, feel secure. We usually achieve those goals by adopting certain behaviors. For example, we can be from a particular area and take on specific styles of dress or ways of speaking, and think we're just being ourselves. We may call it "representing." We rep our neighborhood, our team, our race, our faith, our gender, our career, but somewhere in there, we can easily go from the real to the representative.

We can buy so far into these beliefs about what we appear to represent that we actually start to become uncomfortable when we have to venture out into other spaces. Our representative is more potent than we are because it copes better than we do. But there's this one thing: The rep doesn't like change.

Change is too tricky; change is dangerous. "How would it look if so-and-so caught me acting that way or wearing my hair like that?" we ask ourselves. "How could I explain to so-and-so that I'm working for those people?"

"Nah," we say. "Let's do myself a favor and stick to being who I really am and stay where I'm most accepted." Until one day, we're not. And it's devastating.

Sometimes we're brainwashed into belief systems and placed under laws that have little to do with who we really are and more to do with a plan that we're not always hip to. I've always been fascinated by the deep and sometimes dark unknown, but I'm not talking about conspiracy theories here. I'm talking about the way the world is set up for certain groups to have certain things and others to have less.

This isn't a revolutionary observation, but for those of you who don't know, life isn't set up for fairness. This book isn't about bashing any group or standard of beliefs. We ain't got time for that! I've adopted a growth mindset, and people like me continuously monitor what's going on. But we aim to keep our distance. It's beneficial to our mental health to maintain our internal monologue free from judging ourselves or others. I'm sensitive to both positive and negative information. I'm always searching for where I can take constructive action.

I do me.

Doing you will require confidence. To be an expert at doing you, you have to learn to love, like, and trust yourself. I've become a master at teaching this skill. You see, people tend to tell me all their business, even when I don't ask. This has always been my gift and my burden. Even as a teen, I doled out information to girls in the bathroom who shared their business with me. And since I was a keeper of their secrets, I always felt a particular responsibility to help them.

Today, hundreds of women fill my inboxes, come to my workshops, and hire me as a coach. I love what I do. I love helping others overcome the limitations they place on themselves. I consider myself an expert at conquering my own limiting beliefs. In these pages, I hope to share with you lessons I've learned on the road to recovering from the bullshit I somehow bought into for so many years.

I AM enough. And yes, as a matter of fact, I am too much for some. But guess what? I'm good with that. And if you reach the last page of this book and are good with your brand of extra, my mission will have been accomplished.

I've been involved in some form of spiritual study my entire life. But in addition to not being a guru, I'm not a philosopher or theologian either. I'm just a girl from the neighborhood who always wanted to know why I felt different. So naturally, I started looking for others like me. We are many! Along this journey I've done a lot of research and discovered that everyone learns differently.

Howard Gardner, a Harvard psychologist, said that measuring intelligence based on I.Q. testing is too limited. Having also done research into the controversy of racism in I.Q. testing, I was all ears to learn more. Dr. Gardner's theory states that our schools and culture focus most of their attention on math and reading.

Many children have gifts outside of the traditional, measured boxes and don't receive much reinforcement for them. They sometimes end up being labeled unteachable, unfocused, stupid, challenged, and so much more. So many kids adopt those labels as beliefs and don't realize as they grow into adults that those labels aren't the truth. Imagine how different things would be if we could all feel valued from the beginning of our educational experience. How different might your experience have been?

Here's a final bit of truth for you: You ARE enough, boo. We all are. I don't care if you listen to this on tape because you can't read or if you have a Ph.D. and still feel like a fake. You're the real thing. To quote an author whose works I admire and have explored extensively:

"Today you are you, that is truer than true. There is no one alive who is you-er than you!" - Dr. Seuss.

I have a bit of a potty mouth. Despite that, I consider myself a spiritual person, so I'd like to take a moment here to send you a blessing. From my heart and keyboard, I bless you with good intentions for your day, your week, your life. May you be entertained, enlightened, and just a little more joyful after reading this book.

So no, I'm not a guru, but I am an ambassador of chingonidad, and no matter where you're from, I can already sense that you are, too.

Bienvenidos to my truth, and on to mi vida loca.

# ¡Ey! Where You From?

I HAD NO IDEA this question could spark a war until I moved to Los Angeles. If you picked up this book and know nothing about gang culture, you haven't a clue either. But that's okay. I knew very little about gangs before I met Sad Girl.

I was born at 10 Catherine Slip, a housing project on the Lower East Side of New York City. I'm half Puerto Rican and half Venezuelan, and I was the last born of my parents' four children. My mom kept her pregnancy with me a secret. She had had several miscarriages and she didn't want to have to publicly deal with another.

On the morning of November 11, 1969, as my mom bent over to slip into her pantyhose, her water broke and I started to make my way into the world. My dad delivered me right there, in their bedroom.

I was taken to the hospital and instantly placed in an incubator. None of my siblings had been incubated, so my parents wondered what might be wrong. As they waited for someone to come and inform them, they sat in tense silence until Dad couldn't hold in his confession any longer. In near tears, he told my mom that I was oddly pink and my head was the shape of a football. Mom shrieked in horror and immediately began to blame her age for my abnormality.

It turns out that I was not oddly pink, nor did I have a

football head. I was actually the only white baby in the whole family. Plus, during delivery Dad had pulled my head too hard and squeezed my baby skull into an oblong shape. The nurses had corrected the shape of my head, but that didn't matter to my mom. She still was inconsolable and convinced that I was deformed. A few hours after delivery, a concerned nurse asked my mom why she wouldn't go see her baby. My mom cried, "Because I'm so sad that she's disfigured. It's all my fault, I knew I was too old. Now my poor baby will have to live her life this way!"

Perplexed, the nurse responded, "Ms. Aviles, there's not a thing wrong with your baby. She's as perfect as a baby could be and ready for you to take her home. Let me bring her to you."

And so she did. As my mom would describe it for years to come, I was indeed a perfect baby. All I needed was a name.

As my surprised siblings arrived one by one at the hospital to meet me, everyone pondered a name that would be suitable for this unexpected baby. In the middle of all the discussion, my mom announced that she had had a dream about my name the night before her water broke. She said that in her dream she had actually given birth to a monkey. The monkey shook its fist in her face and insisted on being named Angel Gabriel.

And so I, Angel Gabrielle Aviles, was discharged from the hospital and into the hands of the most eccentric family on the Lower East Side. I went home, back to the projects, where my siblings did the best they could to create an impromptu nursery. I spent the first months of my life in a converted clothes drawer.

Yes, I was a surprise, but I was a dearly loved, strange little white baby girl with a boy's name.

Shortly after my birth, my parents returned to work while my siblings, Val (sixteen), Rick (seventeen), and Rod (twenty), continued on with their busy lives. My mom was working and completing her bachelor's degree. Dad had a decent job, so we moved from the projects into a high-rise co-op across the street. It was definitely a come-up.

After we moved I was sent to my first daycare. Can you believe that I still, to this day, remember moments in my first sitter's house? I recall understanding Italian words and smelling my sitter's home cooking. But most of all, I remember Antoinette, her intellectually disabled daughter. Antoinette would watch over me as I slept. I remember actually feeling the love that came out of her eyes. At the age of three I knew that others treated Antoinette differently, but I didn't know why. As far as I was concerned, she was the loveliest of all. Antoinette was like a real angel to me. It was like she was my kind, and I just knew it.

There weren't a whole lot of our kind around as far as I could tell. As young as four or five I would lie in bed, stare up at the ceiling, and have a talk with God. It wasn't a scary or even unusual thing for me. It was right before I learned the term *God*, but I understood that something loving, broad, and universal was ever-present. Even at that tender age, I felt so close to the spirit and wondered what I was doing here on Earth. I would find myself asking, Why am I on this planet, and how long do I have to stay until I can go back?

I'd tell my mom about these conversations, and she would say, "You're an alien."

Mom wasn't mean, she was just herself. She was actually excited to share this news with me. She thought I was so amazing. And I felt she was … Well, let's just say it was clear to me that she didn't belong here, either.

Don't get me wrong. I loved my mom. I just wondered why she was okay with being known as *la loca* (*the crazy one*). When I was five I came to the conclusion that to survive this place, we surely have to at least fit in. We have to find a way to make people love and accept us. So at a very young age I identified love and acceptance as commodities that I wanted to have. Love and acceptance seem simple enough, right?

Carmen Reyes was born and raised in East Harlem by a single mom and grandmother. Although they were poor, there was a lot of love and ingenuity in the household. Factory work was always brought home so that pennies could be saved for important things, like food and education. On her first day of school, she was excited to have the privilege of learning. She sat quietly in her chair without having a clue about what the nun was saying. Carmen was smart and creative, but Spanish was her first language, and the nun was speeding through her class rules in English. As she looked around the room, she could see all the other students looking their first day best. Carmen suddenly recalled that her grandmother had packed her a special first-day lunch. Without hesitation, she broke out her lunch and began to happily chomp away. Her joy was cut short by the nun, who both reprimanded her and snatched up her food. Carmen was devastated. She went home to her grandmother, who comforted her and explained that schedules were in place to keep things in order. Mom loved her grandmother Wela more than anything. So when Wela told her that she would have to learn English to be the best student, Carmen got right to business. She learned English and became the best student in her class. Upon graduation, the nuns asked Carmen what she wanted to be when she grew up. My mom, with all the innocence and excitement in the world, exclaimed, "I want to go to Harvard!" The nuns chuckled and replied, "Carmen Reyes. Harvard is an all-boys school for the privileged, and you are a girl with minimal means. You are a smart girl. You should think of becoming a secretary!" Now my mom had no problem with secretaries, she did have a problem with dream crushers. At twelve, she found a way to disenroll herself and her sister from that school. The next year, Wela died. Mom attempted suicide and was hospitalized. What my mom witnessed in the hospital fueled her desire to pursue psychology and work in social services. This was also the time that she determined that she would somehow study at Harvard. And in 1976, she did. Carmen Reyes, facing obstacles that seemed impossible to overcome. When people ask me where I'm from, I don't think about zip code, I think about my mom and say, "I'm from a place where nothing is impossible...»

So Carmen did what she had to do and left me with my dad, Mario. He was a brilliant artist and so flipping handsome. He was also a good man. I was kept fed and clean, and my homework was done. In 1975 that was a big deal for a "single" dad, so I want to give him props for that.

Despite all the tasks he did to take care of me, Mario just wasn't really present. We weren't close, so I can only speculate on why my dad was the way he was. I was the last of his four kids, so maybe the man was just tired. Perhaps he didn't know what to do with a little alien girl. Could it also have been that he didn't realize that predators look for the young, the weak, or the lonely?

I'm guessing that he didn't see the change in me. At six, I wasn't drawing hearts and flowers like the other kids; I was drawing skulls and cemeteries. That was because we had moved again when I was five—a move that resulted in me being molested. While in the care of my new sitter, two teenage boys were touching me. It felt good and bad at the same time. I tried to make sense of what was happening in my world. That was when I began to create formulas in my life.

I wish I could tell you how an event like this can twist and turn itself into becoming the cornerstone of a belief system. I mean, that would be something, right? If I could take you step by step through the mind of a young girl, adolescent, and adult

19

and show you how all the bullshit actually piles up, it might help even more people. But I can only share some of what I remember.

So here it goes. In my mind, I had figured out that my mom left me because I was different. I wasn't pretty and brown like everyone else in the neighborhood. I was ugly.

My dad worked and didn't seem super interested in me or our home. Those boys, however, were interested in me—the ugly girl whose own mom wouldn't raise her. At first I was happy for the attention. But as they ordered me to keep secrets, I came to understand that something must be wrong with how they were treating me. Then I went to church and learned that a young lady who doesn't remain pure is considered sinful or separate from God, and I got mad at those boys. I thought that because of what they'd done, I could no longer go and have my alone time with my creator. "From now on," I told myself, "I have to make it in this world alone."

Those boys had taken something precious from me, and I refused to let that happen to me again. This is where the seeds of anger and unworthiness were planted in me. And as I got older and wiser to the violent things that were happening around me. I felt that if a situation ever came up where I was going to be assaulted, I would have to fight till the death. I would kill or be killed. End of story.

And the angry, unworthy seeds grew into beliefs that I held onto for a LONG time.

Belief is a remarkable thing. We make observations about what we believe. And then, to make life a bit easier to figure out, we create these little formulas, or scripts, that play in our subconscious. The scripts take all kinds of complicated circumstances and situations and boil them down into simple, "IF this, THEN that" statements.

For my tribe and me, the script sounds a bit like this:

If THIS happens,
THEN I will be happy/safe/worthy.

We hear, see, or feel things, then a place in our mind takes all the bits of information and makes a story and formula out of it. This is the story that we tend to base our choices on. Now, the story and its formula can make or break us—and THAT is madness—but we keep tweaking them until we can't do it anymore. That time can come when you're eighteen, or it can come when you're eighty, but when it does come, it comes with POWER.

Oh, how often I go back in time to talk to that little girl. I tell her that other people have nothing to do with her value as a human being. I remind her that nothing can separate her from God. I tell her that all she has to do is remember to love herself then, find her tribe, and she'll be safe; she'll be close to home with earth angels.

But the version of me that came up out of that time wasn't looking for angels. She was looking for ways to cope and protect herself. She was beautiful and deadly. She was brutal with her words and often abusive to her body. She was sometimes reckless, and many times the moves she made seemed fearless to others, but really she was always just looking to fear, less.

I think it's important to stress that my neighborhood in the Bronx was not a horrible place, especially when we first got there in the seventies. At that time in New York City, a neighborhood could change from block to block. I lived in a primarily working-class area. Mine was the only apartment building on the block, and the characters who lived there were so colorful. In my building alone, I remember a designer, a couple of single moms, a college student, a crazy Vietnam Vet, an alcoholic, a drug addict, and an activist. I loved my friends. We could wander for miles, and as long as I was home before the streetlights came on, it was all good. On weekends, there was usually a party happening somewhere. And it was guaranteed that food would be delicious and the music was off the charts. Despite economic challenges, my overall feeling while I lived there was that it was a place full of beautiful brown people.

Growing up, I spent a lot of time with my family. The regulars from that time were few but powerful. As an adult recalling some of my memories, I realize that a common denominator for what created my fondest memories was a sense of security. My mom was gone, and I really wanted to feel safe. My particular measure of safety wasn't logical, it was purely based on feeling. In first place was my sister. Then there was Titi Lulu, Titi Helen, and her kids, Abuelita (my paternal grandmother), and Nana (my maternal grandmother).

My sister, who I called Sissy, treated me like her own daughter from the moment I was born until I was about forty-five! To my knowledge, my sister never had a physical fight in her life. To hear my brothers tell it, she was a goody two-shoes, and they were charged with keeping her safe. Sis was smart, she was an excellent student, but she never felt like she got the support she needed at home. My parents fought like cats and dogs, and my sister hated it. She especially hated how strong and controversial my mom was. My mom and Sis were both alphas, and alpha females can only be around one another for so long. A few weeks after my sister turned eighteen, she called my mom to ask her what she was doing on that Thursday. Mom asked why, and Sis announced that she was getting married.

Sissy had met Carlos, a "fresh off the boat" Dominican, with no papers. He was young and poor, and the odds of their match lasting were not good. But my sister is one of the most mentally tough people I have ever met in my life. She married the love of her life at eighteen, and to this day, they are still together. From as early as I can remember, they took me everywhere with them. Sis and Charlie were the closest to "normal people" we had in my family. My sister has always planned everything. When I was eight, Sis gave birth to my niece, Skye. I loved that kid, and when it was time for my sister to go to work, I became her sitter at thirteen. These days it seems crazy to think about a thirteen-year-old babysitting a five-year-old, but it was typical back then. I was honored to help my sister because she'd always done so much for me, and I was inspired by the kind of woman she was. Sis worked hard and smart. She didn't get formally educated until she was in her thirties. Once she did, she didn't stop until she had a double MBA and a management position at a telecommunications company. Charlie was not formally educated, but he was the most incredible example of a man who didn't fear his woman's rise. He actually became the wind beneath my sister's wings. As a kid, you don't pick up on those things, but when you are grown, you recognize what goes into a recipe for success.

Titi Lulu was tough as nails and one of the most complicated people I ever met. She knew many shady people and was the keeper of many secrets, but she would say the craziest shit to people. Her sentences would often begin with "Not for nothing but..." And she'd follow up with something offensive. She loved us profoundly, but we simply couldn't live up to her standards. She would call my mom a pig and bleach every square inch of a perfectly clean apartment. She'd tell me that my dad was trying to make me look homeless and take me shopping. Titi would spare no expense on everything I needed, except shoes. She told me that if she bought me shoes, I would walk out of her life. There were also no hats on the bed, no purses on the floor, and many other rules I could never remember. There was also a list of people you couldn't mention in her house. My aunt had her crazy ways, but she was loyal and would cuss anyone out who messed with her family. She lived in an area of the Bronx that some may have been intimidated by. But I was Lulu's niece, and I felt NO FEAR.

My Titi Helen didn't like my mom or me. She was very religious and judgmental. Fortunately, her kids were not. I especially loved my cousin, Sylvia. Back in the day, adults had no problem sending seven-year-olds to the market. Especially when they were accompanied by their "worldly," nine-year-old cousin. To be fair, even at nine, cuz had swag. No matter where we went, it always felt like she owned the place. We would make our way to the market across the street from the Patterson projects. She would cross Morris Avenue like she was grown and make sure I was in tow. Sylvia was always, what Chicanos call, trucha. Trucha means to be on the lookout. She was the first person to explain why the elevators had mirrors in the corner. She made sure that I understood that I HAD to look in that mirror because someone might be hiding in the corner waiting for me. At five, she informed me that I must not blindly walk into rape, robbery, or abduction. Cuz grew up to work as an officer on Rikers Island.

As a kid, seeing either of my brothers was always a treat. They were both playful and fierce. If you talked to my brother Rod, he would say he was not a fighter. He would say he was the one who always had to fight on behalf of someone else. I get it. Rod wanted to be a hippie. He wanted the easy-going life-style that seemed to flow in areas like Berkeley or Woodstock, but it was harder to come by on the lower East Side. Rod was a peace lover but would often say that a walk on the wrong block could get you in a fight. He moved to Boston when I was three or four. When I was nine, my mom brought me to Boston to live with her while she worked and went to school. I missed my life back in the Bronx, but having my brother close meant the world to me. I would be over the moon when either he or Rick would show up to my school activities. Rod was a handsome and talented guy. His music collection, cooking, and sense of style were always impressive. But what I remember most is him playing with me and suddenly looking at me with teary eyes and saying, "I love you so much, sister! There are only a few people that I would die for. And you are one of them." I have put myself in some fucked up situations, most of which I will not be detailing in this or any other book. I am happy to say that I never had to call upon that service from my brother, but to this day, I believe he still means it.

When mom and I lived in Boston, I was thrilled to be with her, but I was like a fish out of water. Mom was concerned about the quality of education in Boston, so she immediately enrolled in the METCO program. The Metropolitan Council for Educational Opportunity was a school-integration program that bussed thousands of students from predominantly black and Latino neighborhoods to wealthy, white areas in the suburbs. I was sent to a school in a small town called Weston. There were only a handful of black kids and no Latinos at my new school. As far as I could tell, you could be black or white. I chose black, of course, but I was barely brown, so that choice was just another example of an inside-out disconnect.

The resources in Weston were phenomenal, and I was a pretty smart kid. I did well in everything except for a science class that required bird watching. I have a feeling that my teacher was not prepared to deal with students from diverse backgrounds. When I explained that I could not spot certain species on my outings, he seemed to think I was not trying hard enough. He set up a parent/teacher meeting with my mom. Considering my mom had to take public transportation to make the twenty-mile trek to my school, the meeting wrapped up rather quickly. Mr. Birdwatcher curiously retired in the middle of that year. She never told me exactly what was said in that meeting. Whatever it was, the dude was not ready for the likes of Carmen. Nothing shakes a microaggressor more than an educated Latina. Aside from this teacher, a couple of fights and total culture shock, my years in Boston were pretty good.

My first physical altercations happened when I moved to Boston. I remember being such a peaceful kid. But between the anger of holding a secret that separated me from God and suddenly not fitting in anywhere, I found myself fighting for something I'm not sure I understood. Pride? Respect? I was only nine, and in one year, there were two instances. The first happened at school. I was on the swing set with another girl from METCO, my one and only friend at the time. Two girls from the town approached and uttered some slurs. I can't recall what happened from my time on the swing to when I ended up in the Principal's office. The actual fight was a blur. A clump of hair in my hand was the only real evidence of what had transpired.

My next bout happened at an after school program that I attended. This time it was with a girl from Roxbury who decided one day that she didn't like the attention my hair was getting. For a week, she told anyone who would listen that she was going to kick my butt. I was scared shitless. That Friday, I knew that I would have to fight, and I did not want to. As we made our way down the stairs, I could hear the kids tell me how I'd better be prepared to take the whipping. I remember the girl waiting for me at the base of the stairs, in terror and without thinking, I launched myself off the stairs and onto her body. We fought, and I came out without any bruises. I had faced a bully, and the kids cheered me. I was not a fighter, luck and gravity had been on my side. I don't remember being in trouble either by the program administrators or my mom.

I believe I made it through my time in Boston without any further incidents because I was given a chance to be creative. My passion for the arts was fueled by Mom, who would take me to all the performances, museums, galleries, and libraries she could find. My mom was a student, and money was tight. We lived in a one-bedroom apartment on the bus route between Cambridge, where she went to school, and Dorchester, where she worked. Mom was industrious, though, she found every free thing we could do and always scraped together money for my classes.

It was while in Boston that I began ballet classes and received my first paycheck as an artist! The Nutcracker was a big deal at Boston Ballet. Stage moms flurried about, and kids came in all their fanciest dancewear. I auditioned and got a tiny part for which I was paid one dollar per performance. I instantly loved it. I loved rehearsal, enjoyed the stage, loved my hair and make-up, and loved performance time. It was a whole new world for me. I didn't fit in one hundred percent there, but something about it was magical. I could be soft and airy and anything I wanted to be. I was hooked.

In addition to ballet, at school, I was encouraged to play an instrument. My mom suggested I follow in my sister's footsteps and play the flute. A lovely small flute would have been perfect for us on our bus rides. But on the day we were to pick our instruments, I heard a sound I instantly loved. I came home that day with a cello. It never crossed my mind that mom might be terrified something could happen to that big and expensive instrument. Or how I would transport it. I just learned to play. I got into a private school for the arts in Massachusetts, but I couldn't afford to attend. Without missing a beat, Mom and I went back to the Bronx, so I'd have a chance to attend one of the public art schools in New York City.

One evening when I was twelve, I announced that I'd be auditioning for the Performing Arts High School (which soon after became the Fiorello H. LaGuardia High School of Music & Art and Performing Arts). This was the school featured in one of my favorite films, Fame! We were all at dinner, and Mom clasped her hands with delight when I told them what I was planning.

Dad asked, "Why?"

To which, I replied, "I think I'd like to be a dancer."

His response floored me: "Oh, sheez. A dancer? Yeah, right. Keep dreaming!"

It was the first time I remember feeling stabbed emotionally. His words rendered me silent. That line haunted my dad for years because my mom was a lioness, and her cub had clearly been wounded. I was in shock, though I never doubted my dad's love for me. When I excused myself from the table, it was to regroup. I began to imagine my declaration being total foolishness.

This event created a new formula for me.

Formula:

IF I fail,

THEN my dad will not love me.

That formula became the pre-audition script that played in my head. And at EVERY audition I had, I went up against the part of my own ego that disguised itself as my dad's voice: "Keep dreaming, loser. Keep dreaming ... you're not gonna make it."

To which my response was always, "FINE! I WILL keep dreaming. I will get this!"

And so I went into battle, and it was an exhausting but effective process.

I spent hours practicing for my high school audition, and I ultimately made it in. Finally, the weird girl who didn't really fit in anywhere found her place among the other overly sensitive, dramatic, eccentric kids at Performing Arts High School. But now I was called "special, creative, gifted …"

Sadly, I was never really close to my dad again. I believe now that everything in life has a purpose and meaning.

I once interviewed Oliver Stone. He said every filmmaker has to be a bit mad; it doesn't make sense to devote a lifetime to an art form, not even to the artist compelled to make it.

My dad sold insurance to keep us fed, but he was always an artist. His work hung all about the house. So I couldn't understand why he'd responded to my desire for self-expression in such a discouraging way. If I had to bet, I would say it was fear. Have you ever had someone who loved you but was so afraid of life that they tried to protect you in a way that ended up hurting you?

After that incident at the dinner table, I never shared my dreams or plans with my dad again. The truth is that my confidence was always too fragile to go up against his fear-filled reality. It took me thirty years, but because of the healing work I've done, I was finally able to let my dad off the hook. I love him. He did the best that he could with the formulas he was working with. Now when I think of him, I say, "THANK YOU, Dad!"

Somewhere along this journey, it finally occurred to me that regardless of where his fear came from, I got to make art for a living because he didn't. He worked a steady job not because he loved it but because it was the right thing for a guy with a family to do. As a young Puerto Rican kid, he wasn't afforded the same opportunities I was. He wasn't encouraged or given classes or any of the many tools needed to make a living doing what he loved. So there he was, this artist stuck in a life that didn't include using his talent.

Every day I would travel an hour on the train from the Bronx to school. The Bronx in the eighties had really lost its luster. Crack was coming up everywhere, and many families had moved. My building in particular fell into a sad state. I remember one year, our building didn't have enough heat to combat the draft coming through our old, single-pane windows. My parents covered our windows with bubble wrap.

I was embarrassed by my home and detested the fighting between my parents. So I focused even more on art. I was a dance major, which exposed me to music and drama, and it was there, in those classes, that I found my refuge. Creative expression and the discipline involved in maintaining what was required to consider a career in the field was a powerful combination. It kept me from a lot of things I might have gotten into had I just been left alone with my insecurities and anger.

I went on to Hunter College, but I dropped out after a year. To support myself, I worked in bars and clubs and got an agent right away. I worked as an actor in New York, but it soon became evident that if I was going to pursue acting full time, I would have to move to Los Angeles. So in 1992, I packed my bags and split. It's a good thing I left when I did because the club scene at that time was crazy. For me, drinking and drugs had become a regular activity. Alcohol related brawls were not uncommon.

I hit the ground running when I got to Los Angeles. I know I was running, but from what? I couldn't tell you, because frankly, I'd put the molestation way outside my mind. I no longer drank or took drugs, and I had cut off toxic and code-pendent relationships. I felt renewed, focused and determined. I guess I was running toward opportunity. I was simply making the moves I had to make and saying yes to the opportunities that presented themselves. My first audition season in Los Angeles was busy. Every audition I aced allowed me to move closer to my formula of achievement.

Formula:

If I work as an actress,

THEN I will be happy/worthy/loved.

Life was good in Los Angeles. I was one of a handful of Latina actresses who consistently booked film, television, and commercial work. I was able to work on projects with some of the most prolific and talented minds in the industry at that time. Obviously, the most pivotal role of all was that of Sad Girl. She's an icon, and it's almost surreal to live in her body. I've done meet-and-greets where people waited for hours to meet her and tell her their stories. I had no idea at the time about the kind of impact this movie would have for genera-tions to come. NONE. I didn't know that having the guts to pursue my dreams would lead thousands of girls to see them-selves in me and be inspired to create dreams of their own.

Most people who know about the film want to know what it was like to work on that set. For those who don't know about the film, it takes place in an area of Los Angeles known as Echo Park and is a hybrid cast of actors and real gang members. We were all blessed to be in a movie directed by Allison Anders, an incredibly talented artist, and an inspiring human. At first, I was intimidated to work with the gang because, to be honest, most of what I knew about the life was from the media. Half the news stories that came out of South Central or East Los Angeles were about a drive-by or carjacking. I'm not saying that violence didn't exist, I am saying that the press didn't paint a full picture of life as it was happening. I grew up around crime and violence, but I also grew up around a lot of love, and that's precisely what I found in Echo Park.

When we had our first meeting, the Locas looked at us like, "You have to be kidding! These scrawny broads are not fit to come in here and play one of us." But we were bound and determined to bring it. By the wrap of the movie, most of us were crying. We were all exhausted, but we had spent months together. And we had been committed to each other and to sharing a broader perspective of barrio life.

Allison Anders said she knew I was her Sad Girl from the moment I walked into the audition. I'll never forget that she said that there was an air of melodrama about me. Melodramas are known to be excessively sentimental. I wanted that for Sad Girl; she was written that way. I wanted it to be hard for people to hate her, despite the mistakes that she had made. Let's be honest, Sad Girl committed one of the worst crimes a female can commit within her circle. She got involved with her best friend's man. I needed to portray how conflicted she was to fall in love. I needed to show how this girl, despite all her crazy experiences, could still be innocent in so many ways. I wanted people to relate to her struggle. I wanted people to see how complicated life was for Sad Girl, beyond the labels she chose or was given.

I didn't need to have been in a gang to understand the desire to be protected and accepted. My intention was not to romanticize gang life. My intention was to humanize a character who could have easily, on paper, seemed like a monster. The reality is that it's easy to judge, ostracize, and stigmatize the poor, but poverty itself is the real criminal. And poverty is systemic, rooted in economics, politics, and discrimination. It doesn't matter where in the world you are from, there will always be more violent crime where poverty is present. I am asked all the time if I am still in touch with members of the cast. Absolutely. I still talk to some of the original Locas, as well as some of the actors. It was an extraordinary project.

Some of the highlights of my career outside of *Mi Vida Loca* were:

*Desperado* with Salma Hayek and Antonio Banderas. (Trivia) Salma had been in Mi Vida Loca and actually recommended me to Robert for that role.

*Scorpion Spring* with Esai Morales and Matthew McConaughey. (Trivia) Midway through the shoot, my appendix ruptured, and I almost died. The sound engineer and producer saved my life.

*Awakenings* starring Robert De Niro and Robin Williams. Directed by Penny Marshall. (Trivia) Don't look for me in this film because my part ended up on the cutting room floor. I was twenty and cast as the wife of a cab driver that helps Robert De Niro. The character is a young mom, and they were looking for her son. I suggested they take a look at my nephew Lorenzo, who was four and looked just like me. He was cast in the film and did a fantastic job. Immediately, my sister was asked to bring him to an agency. Lorenzo didn't impress the agent. He was asked to do an apple pie commercial to which he grumpily replied, "I hate apples!" This line marked the end of his career but gave the family a lot of laughs. I was upset to learn I had been cut out of the award-winning film, but Penny Marshall was golden. Months before the movie released, I received a note from her, apologizing for the cut. That doesn't usually happen in Hollywood, but Ms. Marshall cared about people.

A couple of episodics, including a special episode of *ER* by Quentin Tarantino. (Trivia) Some of the most precise, and physical work I ever had to do as an actor. You can see a portion of this episode on Youtube.

A pilot for Fox, directed by Michael Patrick King, known as the writer and producer for Sex and The City. (Trivia) This part was initially written for a Kate Moss type. I couldn't have been further from Kate Moss if I tried, so I went in as "Marisol," a homegirl from the Bronx with an attitude. Boom. They loved her. That show never got picked up, but I am writing about this because it was a big deal for me. Women of color were not walking into Network meetings and taking over roles intended for white women.

Multiple Commercials. (Trivia) The best commercial job I ever booked was actually before Mi Vida Loca. It was for Diet Coke, and it was shot in Japan!

Multiple Voice Overs, including background-voice work for the film 187. (Double Trivia) I was insecure about my voice because, as a young actress, I had been told it was a weakness. I booked jobs because I learned how to work my voice, and I quickly picked up dialects. If you'll recall, Sad Girl narrates quite a bit of Mi Vida Loca. The crazy thing about 187 is that I auditioned for a role in the film, and it was one of the last auditions of my career. I did not get the part, but when I got to the studio to work in post-production, I was excited to see that my friend from high school, Karina Arroyave had booked the job!

The craziest job ever. I had my pregnant belly cast for the movie Twins, starring Danny DeVito and Arnold Schwarzenegger. That baby kicking in Arnold's belly is modeled after my daughter!

Yes, the nineties were a truly spectacular time for me. Not only was I creatively expressing myself, but I also met one of the great loves of my life, my daughter Ariana. I had met her dad, Rico, at the Roxbury nightclub. He was an athlete, and although he was trained to deal with all kinds of potential problems in a cool, calm, and collected manner, I recognized a lingering element of thug in him. I can't fully explain it, but his hood vibe was familiar and, therefore, attractive to me. We were both neighborhood kids who found ourselves able to float around in worlds outside where we came from. Neither of us really fit in anywhere, but we kind of fit together. I was cute, and he was this handsome, giant black man, with a kind heart, and killer smile. He was a protector and would NEVER let anything happen to his offspring, or me. In my mind, he was the perfect person to have a baby with.

Soon after Ari was born, I lost one of the great loves of my life—my brother Rick. Coping with Rick's death wasn't easy. I had never lost someone I was close to before. Not only was he my brother, but he was also my career mentor, my chief cheerleader, my prime example of how to go out there and claim my shit. He instilled confidence in me because I knew his love for me was unconditional. Rick Aviles had literally taken himself from the streets of New York City to a Hollywood success story right before my eyes.

Rick had been a heroin addict for most of his life, and it wasn't until the eighties that he was able to shake the disease. He was so flawed, so broken in a million little pieces, but so talented and brave. Without him, I had a new kind of fear. I doubted myself. Suddenly the rejection from ten auditions was too much.

There's no other way to put it: Death is a mutha-fucka. My brother's death was earth-shattering for me. When you're in a situation, it's hard to see that the moves you're making to protect yourself are actually leading you to a place that is further away from where you long to be.

Formula:
IF I live a normal life,
THEN I will be stable and eliminate the risk of pain.

Rico and I got married, and I went back to school for multimedia production. I learned to use a nonlinear editor, which at the time was a big deal. Robert Rodriguez used it on the set of *Desperado*, which made the filmmaking process ten times faster. So many people ask me why I left acting. While I still loved the craft, the entertainment industry is a business, and I no longer wanted to be in it. Truth be told, I was terrified of being a mom, and I didn't think I could do both. I could have gone into a more creative production environment, but I just wanted a regular life—one that didn't demand the everyday rigor of being on my A-game. I got a nine-to-five job right after school and worked in mediocre employment for years. My only creative outlet was a blog my friend Paul and I co-created. We focused on highlighting artists in the Latino community. It was all good, though, because my family was growing. After Ari, we had two additional and amazing kids. My Trinity came to me as a gift in 2001, and Kross followed twenty months later.

With three kids, a full-time job, a house, responsibilities at church, and the ever-present need to still look good as a wife in Los Angeles, life was busy. But I had a system. And my mom was a huge part of that system. Rick's death had taken a toll on her. She was still active but not as loud and crazy as she had been when I was a kid. My kids loved her. Mom would take them, and more than that, she would just offer me a spot where I could veg out. I know that she knew how tired I was, and I think she suspected that the subtle betrayals I had committed against myself would somehow catch up to me. But Mom was a trained therapist. Some days she would ask me questions, and some days she would just let me flop on her couch and sleep.

Carmen Reyes Aviles had spent many years being painfully smarter than the people around her. She had an inherent understanding of what it cost to do you as a woman, and she had paid the hefty price. There was a total non-judgmental component to her character. She could quickly identify the differences in people, but she didn't insert her opinions unless she was asked. I think this is one of the things that made her so special. It's so frustrating when you're not able to fully understand the magnificence of someone until they're gone. I mean, don't get me wrong: I was the one in my family charged with taking care of Carmen. I bought a place with a front unit so that she could live out her years close to the people she loved. But, to be honest, I didn't fully grasp all the things she'd been teaching me all along. Not until she was gone.

That day came when I was thirty-five and Mom had a massive stroke.

Carmen had always said that if her brain was not in one hundred percent working order, she was done. She didn't want to just be a body taking up space. I'll tell you that, although I loved my mom and wanted to fulfill her wishes, when it came down to pulling a plug, I couldn't do it.

I visited her in the hospital every day for three months. My already burdened schedule had gone up a notch to accommodate the newly acquired job of staying on top of my mom's healthcare. The truth is that I wasn't sure how I would make it without her. I was once again stuck in this feeling of utter terror. I know I looked independent to everyone else, but my mom was a pillar of strength for me. She was who I could go to when I just needed to cry. Sometimes a grown-ass woman needs that space. It's not a space to get fixed; it's just a place to sit and be real.

But over those three months, I grew the strength to let my mom go. One afternoon, I went to visit her. I prayed and didn't ask God to bring her back. I didn't ask her to fight and get strong enough to come home. Instead, I told her that I was okay. That we would all be okay. And that if she wanted to leave, I was strong enough to let her go.

Before I even made it home from the hospital, she was gone.

I was about my word, though! I went into full-on survival mode. Man, you should have seen me then. Still looking fabulous with my beautiful brown family. Still trying to appear like I had all my ducks in a row. It was all good until I was thirty-eight and had my first panic attack.

I was at Disney World with my family, having the time of my life. But then I got on a ride that changed my life. Finding myself barely able to make it on the flight back to California was the beginning of my descent into a few very dark years. I found myself not only physically unable to do simple things like ride in an elevator or handle even small crowds, but also questioning everything I had, everything I knew, everything I was, and everything I believed.

After my mom died, we started a construction project in my home that never got completed. I lived in a work zone for years, and it was horrible. In addition to living in a place I hated, I had a ton of debt from a home equity loan. I tried to be grateful for what I had, but living like that brought back the feeling of being embarrassed about my home, flashbacks of being molested, and feelings of unworthiness. It was a nightmare.

Contrary to what I had imagined my life would be at forty, I found myself in a perpetual state of sadness. I was always in fear that a panic attack would strike. And because I was utterly terrified of medication, I was continually looking for natural potions and cures for anxiety and depression. I remember getting dressed to go to a friend's wedding and then not being able to get in my car because I was afraid of the drive.

How could this be happening to me? Life wasn't perfect, but at least I had all my bases covered, didn't I? I was married to the father of my three beautiful kids. We went to church and

I served my community. I had my own business. I was in good health. What could possibly be missing? Why did I feel like I was an extra in my own life?

I could never put my finger on it, but IT was ever present. IT was this sublime mediocrity, settling, waiting—these are all terms for a condition I now simply call sleep.

All these balls were in the air. I was juggling all the items that I needed to complete my happy formula, but something in my core was asleep. I thought back to the many compromises I had made—and that one little decision I had made to choose a life that didn't require me to be on my A-game. I had chosen a path that I thought would be easier, but it wasn't! I was working super hard for a life that wasn't in full agreement with my purpose. I had chosen a life that highlighted others more than myself, and I had come to believe that was the way it was SUPPOSED to be.

I had adopted and created a culture in which a woman was supposed to put herself last. Well, my choosing mediocrity came with a cost. I'm not here to tell you that other people haven't made similar choices and weren't not living full out. How could I possibly know what someone else's truth is? All I can do is share my experience with you.

What I found on this journey was MY truth.

I was awakened. This awakening came with traumatic results, including the loss of a marriage, home, and connection to friends and family. Many onlookers claimed I was "crazy," "selfish," or "going through a midlife crisis." I remember tweeting, "This is not a midlife crisis, it's a midlife REVELATION!"

On many days my revelation felt like a crisis. It was a brutally lonely time, but it was also a time when I humbly went searching for help. To salvage my sanity, I had to unlock my heart and open my mind.

It took a few years for me to ultimately be free of the panic attacks, but I can honestly say that I'm grateful to have experienced them. Those attacks made me hypersensitive to how I live my life. Today I ride on planes, get in elevators, and even manage to get on SOME amusement park rides. I travel the world. I share my truth in the form of workshops and speaking engagements. I get to help people from all walks of life. One day you may see me in a prison, the next I may be speaking to an audience of business owners, influencers, actors, students, you name it.

Life is far from mediocre. If you're where I've been or feel like you may be getting there, stay in these pages. This book is designed to help. It's not a replacement for your doctor, spouse, church, or school. It's merely a compilation of things I've learned along my journey. Every chapter addresses the healing I found in awakening to life as I see it.

Or more accurately, life as I currently choose to experience it.

I don't care if you've failed a million times before, or if you've tried this or that because other people told you you should do something. You're here for a reason, and you can learn pretty much anything you put your mind to.

It's okay to not want to change or to not be ready for change. Preparation sometimes takes time. If you don't like anything you learn here, you can always go back to your old way of living, with my blessing and best wishes. There are physical, mental, emotional, and spiritual components tied to what's in this book. I sometimes make religious references from multiple sources. I wish to offend no one. I only ask that you approach with an open mind and suspend personal belief systems just long enough to let some of your possibilities percolate.

I literally tore my belief system down to re-establish a very personal relationship with my creator. This relationship is not up for scrutiny or argument, nor do I push it on others as an agenda. Trust and believe that I've had to battle some incredible forces to come to peace with that. It's my sincere desire that you come to harmony with your own organic beliefs. The hardest battle was always within my own mind, but I came to love myself and my life more than ever.

I broke free from mediocrity and, indeed, became too happy to be Sad Girl! How did I do it? In the following chapters I share with you the modalities of wellness that transformed my life. I hope that if you're anywhere near where I was, you'll find some useful tools in these pages.

# Letting Go To Grow

## How surrender and forgiveness lead to freedom.

ORIGINALLY HAD THIS chapter as the last in the book. But although there's no particular order to these chapters, I felt it best to move this one to a primary position. Let me give you a bit of backstory.

Frankly, what's in this chapter is, by far, the most important thing I've learned in my life. And I'm pretty sure that if this is the only thing you learn in this entire book, it can change your life, too.

It was sometime around 2009, and I was in a particularly bad state of mind. My then husband and I were fighting and I was beyond done. This section is a painful thing for me even to write because today I love this man like a brother. He's a good man and the father of my children. But this book is about sharing my truth, so I'll confess that there were many times that I fucking hated him! It's so sad how you can love someone one minute and then hate their guts another.

*Hate* is such a harsh word. It's such an ugly word, but it's real. There is hate in the world and, sadly, it can make a home inside us. There's a whole truth about that time, which is this: What I hated was the fact that I felt trapped inside a life that I had settled for but not one that I wanted to live. I loved

God, I loved my family, but I didn't love me. I wasn't aware of that until later. So for most of this dark time, I spent my days trying to avoid who I thought was the main contributor to my misery: Rico.

I had been with him for a long time, and for over seventeen years we loved each other but we'd also said and done many horrible things to one another. I don't want to paint a false picture; my marriage was not an abusive one. Rico was a bodybuilder, and as big as that man ever got, he never put his hands on me. I'm glad shit never went down like that because, as I mentioned, I could be a bit volatile, especially around the time of my pregnancies.

We got into it once while I was pregnant with my first daughter. I was so enraged that I tried to run him off the road. Truth be told, this was not a massive departure from my non-pregnant behavior. I didn't have the tools I needed to deal with the many emotions I was processing. Pregnancy made me feel weaker than I was used to being, and I hated it. I would feel disrespected or disappointed, but I couldn't figure out how to fix these things in a productive way. I would instead find myself rolling up on a three hundred pound, ex-gangster, who would look at me like I had lost my damn mind. He'd walk away to avoid conflict and inevitably end up in a situation that would make me feel even more disrespected.

During our youthful years together, we were more often at odds than not. Although Rico never hit me, he didn't fall short on temper, either. I'm grateful that our fights didn't escalate beyond what they did. Rico had grown up in South Los Angeles. Early on in our relationship, he made it clear that he was not to be disrespected. I was from New York, I also made it clear that I was not to be disrespected. That seems like a basic set of rules to follow, right? It's not, especially when dealing with young, immature people. It took us years to learn how to speak to one another without being utterly offensive. Once we had our baby, she became the center of our love, and we built tolerance and respect for one another around that.

Over the years, we both changed significantly. We matured. We did grow to love one another, and then we grew apart. What I have since discovered is that we weren't unlike many other married couples. We were in a marriage with kids and responsibilities, and we communicated on a very superficial level. We did what we could to move swiftly past pain, disappointment, and even the worst kinds of betrayal. When we were married, we were committed to never speaking about divorce. We forgave each other, swept issues under the rug, ignored problems, and forgot about many things for many years

To be honest, there were years when I was too busy to pay much attention to how I felt about life. In my thirties, life was so busy. I didn't have time for deep feelings, which was fine because I had come to believe that my feelings were a distraction and likely to get me in trouble. I kept things upbeat and light. Deep emotions were just obstacles blocking the progress toward my goals. I guess, in a way, I thought that eventually I would arrive at my goal—when I had some grandkids and I could proudly share how I had a fifty-year-old marriage. I don't know what made me think that time was an indicator of success, but the truth is that I did.

At some point I thought that happiness was a fleeting thing, so I decided that I shouldn't place too much value on it. Somewhere in there I replaced being happy with being grateful. I want to emphasize that it was gratitude that kept me alive. I was thankful for everything. Still, there was an emotional experience missing. During this time, waves of anxiety and depression would hit me. Some days I felt the burden of sadness so intensely that I couldn't get out of my closet.

If I expressed my feelings, Rico might comment, "But you have so much to be grateful for."

*Yes!* I would think to myself. *But what do I do with this darkness? It's eating me up!* I thought about these words, but I didn't give them life outside my mind. I stayed quiet and focused on being grateful.

As regular folks, we don't get advanced training on how to sit with someone's grief or pain. I'm so grateful for the doctors, therapists, and coaches out in the world, doing the work. Today I know that I can be thankful, even in sadness. Gratitude is a state of being that can coexist with others. You can bless a hungry child with a delicious orange and watch as her eyes well with tears of gratitude. She's grateful, but it doesn't mean that she's full. A son who loses a parent can be thankful for the relationship and still feel the devastation of loss. We're complex beings, and our emotional well-being should include being able to make our way through the many layers of what we feel. Sometimes we need the distraction, and sometimes we need to let wounds heal.

Again, as simple as that sounds, I didn't know it then.

I realize now that living a happy life is a very first-world concept. So many people, especially women, don't have the privilege of looking into what will make them happy. So I consider it such an honor to have been given a chance to pursue my emotional freedom and happiness. During what I now call my "breakthrough era," I felt like I was fighting for my life. I was beyond being able to repair what had broken in my marriage. I was hopeless, afraid, and brokenhearted— and I just detested the way I was living. So I set about to find out exactly what the problem was. I was sure whatever I found would be all Rico's fault.

I'm going to tell you a secret. When you set your mind to look for something, eventually you'll find it. I found fault after fault, which just fueled my anger and gave me more excuses to distance myself emotionally from my husband.

## "I SAT WITH MY ANGER LONG ENOUGH, UNTIL SHE TOLD ME HER REAL NAME WAS GRIEF."

### – AUTHOR UNKNOWN

During one of my random investigations, I remember being particularly enraged about something. I stood in my shower, scrubbing my body nearly raw. Coming out of the shower, I realized that I had no towel, which just added fuel to my fire. I picture myself now, running through the disaster that was my house, naked, dripping wet from the shower, and screaming at the top of my lungs, "I HATE YOU!" I'm so very grateful that no one else was there to witness what must have looked like total madness.

I think I have to elaborate a bit on my home because I believed it was one of the sources of my depression. I had so desperately wanted a house I could be proud of, something that would erase the feeling of shame I had felt while living at my dad's place in the Bronx. I didn't know then that shame is an inside job. I didn't know that you attract what you fear. Despite doing everything in my power to move past my past, there it was, waiting for me.

When my brother died he had left me a small inheritance, and I had spent every penny on buying my house. It was just a little duplex in a working-class neighborhood of Los Angeles, but I was so proud of that house. It was both my nest egg and an homage to my brother. My mom lived in the first house, and I lived in the back with my family. While mom was alive, we would tackle projects together, like ripping out the front yard and replacing the grass with succulents. As Mom aged and

I got busier with work and kids, the house got harder to take care of, but it was still home.

When Mom died, I wanted to sell the house. It was painful to come home and not see her in the front window, which is a perfect example of me shutting down that inner voice. It killed me a little bit every day to drive up to my house and not see my mom, but I didn't fight to protect that part of me. Instead of selling, I was convinced that renovating would be best for my family. We started the construction, but years later we had no money to finish. So there I was, living in a dirty hellhole of a place where nothing worked as it should. The house was a dangerous maze of exposed plumbing, wires, and giant holes in the floors. I had always been terrified of rats, and during this time rats had made homes under the house. At night, I could hear them squeaking and scratching in the roof and garage. This situation was not about me living in a messy house. It was about me attracting and living in my nightmare.

On this revolutionary day, as I ran around the house screaming and naked, the kids were at school and Rico was wherever he was. I was alone, and I just needed to let out the years of hate and hurt that seemed trapped inside my body. In my fury, I flew down the hall and tripped down the makeshift stairs that led to our bedroom. I landed painfully on the bare, concrete floor—the same one that my daughter had cracked her teeth on a few years before. On this day, my teeth were spared, but my knees and shin were severely scraped. I'm pretty sure that had I not been alone, this would have been a 5150. (For non-Californians, that's the code for being placed in a mental facility.) I ugly-cried, naked, on the floor for what seemed like hours until a phone call disrupted my indulgent release.

On the line was a friend calling to check on me. I had known this woman for years, but life had taken us down separate roads for a while. We had recently reconnected and she knew I was struggling, so she called often. She could hear over the phone that day the state of mind I was in, so she told me to get dressed and meet her at a nearby coffee shop. I was a bleeding, puffy-eyed *mocosa* (translates to *snot-nosed one*), but I went to meet her.

We had lunch and she listened to me pour out both my wrath and my pain. If you have one person in the world who you can sit and share your ugly tears with, you're a lucky soul. I must've stored up some karmic points somewhere because I scored big on that day.

With all the love in the world, my friend looked at me and said, "You know I feel you, girl, but there's only one move you can make from here. You have GOT to forgive your husband!"

"I have forgiven him, and I work on it every day!" I quickly responded.

"You help everyone around you," she said. "You listen and serve and rescue everybody around you, but you're mad, and you're exhausted. Physician, heal thyself!"

If anyone else had said this to me, I might have run out of the place screaming. But this advice came from a woman whom I'd known since before I was married. I felt broken, but I trusted that she saw something fixable in me. And I took heed. I guess it had finally sunk in that I was in a crisis. The truth is that she was the third person who had told me to forgive Rico. Three people had seen in me this thing that I couldn't see for myself. Three people had held up a mirror, but I couldn't see myself until I was ready. I was so sick with anger and grief that I was unrecognizable.

I cried in my car all the way home because I didn't know where to start. I can't say that I was excited about my assignment, because it's hard to be hopeful when you genuinely believe you've tried everything. However, one of the great things about looking for answers inside yourself is that there are endless nooks and crannies to explore.

At this point, I was tired of being miserable, angry, and anxious, so I was willing to try.

When I got home, I just prayed. I thought I had done the work, but now I was humbled by my lack of knowledge. I looked down at my scraped-up knees. I laughed a bit at myself and thought, *This is where my rushing has gotten me. I need to slow down. Whatever happens in my marriage, I need to forgive first. However long it takes. I won't truly move past all this unless I do.*

Then I asked myself a profound question: *What is it that I'm so damn angry about?* I began to write down a list of unspoken atrocities. The list took days to finish, and it was long.

In writing that list, I realized that I had a few things twisted about forgiveness. I believe now that I knew what forgiveness looked like, but not what it was—and I didn't know what it wasn't. The actress knows how to act, but behavior alone isn't forgiveness. Not speaking about feelings isn't forgiveness. Pretending shit didn't happen isn't forgiveness. Ignoring pain isn't forgiveness. Staying in a marriage because that's what's expected of you isn't forgiveness.

For years I was okay with not looking too deeply into feelings or details. I thought I could be free by dismissing all heartache—by dismissing everything. I just wanted to escape the pains of loss, judgment, loneliness, and fear.

But, once again, if you go looking for something, you'll find it. When I went looking for all that I needed to forgive, I found this:

*I forgive you for not thinking about me first with your time, energy, or money.*
*I forgive you for not seeing what I needed.*

*I forgive you for thinking small.*

*I forgive you for not knowing me.*

*I forgive you for trying to hide things from me.*

*I forgive you for trusting others more than me.*

*I forgive you for not acknowledging how amazing I was as a girl or how much MORE amazing I am now.*

*I forgive you for being narrow-minded.*

*I forgive you for hating my tears.*

*I forgive you for not considering my dreams important.*

*I forgive you for not knowing how to be romantic.*

*I forgive your lack of intimacy.*

*I forgive you for planning things last minute and making me feel unimportant.*

*I forgive you for being you and NOT who I thought you could or should be.*

*I forgive you for loving me to the best of your ability; I just want more.*

*I forgive your insecurity.*

*I forgive your imperfections, blindness, and humanity.*

*It all basically boils down to one thing, which is the biggest thing of all: I forgive your fear.*

Please don't get me wrong. I'm not trying to paint a picture that my life was all crap. As a matter of fact, some views of it were lovely. For instance, I was keeping up my life as a fit, working mom of three beautiful kids who went to a prestigious school in Los Angeles. From that perspective, one could argue that my life was enviable. It's just that a part of me was dying. As a matter of fact, during one AWFUL conversation I had with Rico, he looked at me and stated, "We said till death do we part." To which I replied, "I did die. It's just that you didn't notice!"

I hadn't noticed either. What's worse is that I was the killer all along.

It's so hard to explain how the compromises we think we have to make can, ever so subtly, begin to choke the life out of us. How—in order to keep the peace, not rock the boat, and be a "good" person, parent, Christian, wife, friend, or whatever we're trying to be—we muffle a real, living part of ourselves.

I traded one version of myself for someone who was much more agreeable and, therefore, more acceptable. With that trade, the feelings of anger, bitterness, and a burning desire to flee began to build. Soon also came the feelings of guilt, anxiety, and failure. Forgiveness provided a way for the two separate Angels to come together and let me live.

This version of me is not always agreeable or acceptable, but she's also not so full of rage that she will burn her life down.

I thought I had written that letter of forgiveness to and about someone else. But in a sudden moment of clarity, I realized that it was actually to me, and about me. That letter of forgiveness from my higher self was the beginning of a shift inside me. Remarkably, the change came with a measure of compassion and empathy that was utterly unexpected.

And so powerful was that shift that it ultimately diminished the hate and anger I felt towards Rico, my parents, the abusers from my past, the judges in my present, and, most importantly, myself. I wasn't aware that hate, although such a volatile and robust word, has a purpose in life. Hate is a red flag. It's a sign that can function as a fuel or a motivator for change, but I hadn't been taught how to deal with or process it. I'd come to believe that it was shameful to hate. I thought that to be a good person I was supposed to just forgive and love everyone.

So what is forgiveness, really? There was a study done in the eighties about the scientific outcome of forgiveness. The researchers began by defining what the term *forgiveness* means. The definition was a composite of the prevailing ideas presented in both ancient religion and modern philosophical thought. Here's what they came up with: Forgiveness happens when a person who's unjustly treated by others STRUGGLES to abandon resentment and offer kindness or grace toward the unjust.

Did I just capitalize the word *struggle*? Yes, I did. The very definition of forgiveness is about the battle. Now, I needed to know this because my understanding of forgiveness was incomplete. In fact, there are many ways to process forgiveness, and each method is valid. Forgiveness is not about condoning, excusing, forgetting, or even reconciling with another person. What science discovered, and I'm totally paraphrasing here, is that forgiveness is more like a living thing in that it adapts to conditions and circumstances.

Relationships are hard. There are always going to be compromises, but I learned that I have to value myself. Our need to value ourselves comes up in so many areas in life: our personal relationships, our ability to ask for what we deserve at work, or as business owners and artists.

Every time I feel my temper flare up now, I try to look at where I'm making compromises in my own valuation. Compromises have been a huge source of my resentment, bitterness, and anger—all contributors to that big, ugly bucket of hate. The biggest blessing that could come to me is recognizing that when I hate something, there's a reason for it. That reason may look like it exists outside me, but I'm no longer fooled by appearances. Instead, I turn to me.

Hate desires change, and I'm the only person who can truly change how I experience life. When I forgive someone else,

I'm not giving them permission to be an ass, but I am letting their humanity be what it is. To me, forgiveness means I'm not expecting someone to pay a price that may be too high for them. I'm simply paying myself what I'm worth.

I don't care how other people perceive my marriage. My own daughter once told me that my marriage was a failure. That was her opinion at the time, and she's more than entitled to have one. But I grew up in that marriage, and I grew out of it. I birthed three of the human beings I enjoy most in the world. I don't view that as a failure. My marriage became a success when I learned to forgive Rico for what he was and what he wasn't and learned to forgive myself for wanting more.

Forgiveness is the only energy I know that can transform hate (discomfort and the desire for change) into loving action. For me, real forgiveness is a daily practice, and as a hot-tempered, creative Scorpio, I'm given chances to forgive regularly. I'm ten years out from that letter of forgiveness, and I haven't stopped studying forgiveness.

Over these last ten years I've learned that:

1. Forgiveness is a deeply personal experience.
2. You can't forgive by proxy. In other words, you can't do it for someone else and expect real results.
3. Forgiveness can look both selfish and selfless from the outside, so it's super important that you be in constant contact with your higher self.
4. Forgiveness is sometimes like planting a garden. Beautiful plantings may bloom in spring, but they still require pruning and weeding for sustainable results.
5. Forgiving others usually means forgiving yourself too, and that's freedom.

Today if you Google *forgiveness and health*, you'll come up with all kinds of articles. I came across one that said people who reported higher levels of forgiveness also tended to report decreased levels of depression, anxiety, and anger. Go figure! I'm no expert on forgiveness, but I do believe it's one of the keys to my own physical, emotional, and even financial health. If you're struggling in any of those areas, I highly recommend you look at where you need to start doing some forgiving.

Forgiveness is like medicine. It may taste disgusting at first, but it's a real cure. If you've been holding on to past hurts, you can learn to let them go. It may not be easy, but you're worth it.

In the space provided or in a separate journal, take some time to write down any lingering pain or disappointment you're holding on to.

What things have you been angry about?

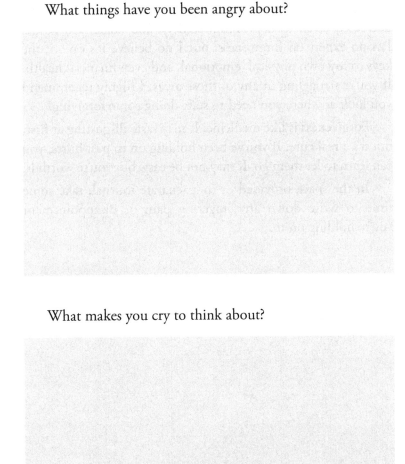

What makes you cry to think about?

Now ask yourself if you're willing to forgive. Willingness plays a huge role in transformation. If you're willing, a way will become clear. End this exercise with the phrase I AM WILLING TO FORGIVE!

# Learning To Be Quiet

## Resting the mind can mend the soul.

I've RUN INTO many people who say they can't meditate because they can't keep their mind quiet. Trust me, my mom introduced me to meditation when I was sixteen, and I wasn't ready. I wanted to smoke weed in Central Park. I didn't want to hang out in a room that smelled like Nag Champa and was full of middle-aged white folks.

Flash forward thirty years, and meditation has become a key ingredient to maintaining my sanity. The irony! The idea that meditation is for a certain kind of person is way too limited. Meditation offers benefits to the entire world! If you've ever come to any of my workshops or worked one-on-one with me, you'll have done some sort of meditation. I love that you can walk into a room full of tatted cholos and see them doing breath work. Some days you might find me meditating with a client across international timelines. Other days you might spot me walking into a juvenile facility or a shelter to share a gift that, once mastered, no one can ever take away.

Throughout this book I try to share with you the way my mind works. Like many of you out there, I have a busy life. I may have had the opportunity to do a few special things, but for the most part my everyday life is full of the same challenges and chores that other moms, business owners, and busy chingonas around the world deal with.

I tend to compartmentalize parts of my life so that I can focus and get through the busiest patches. Mom mode puts me in a space where I can make dinner, tackle questions, emotionally connect, discipline, and organize calendars. Work mode for me is being online 70 percent of the time, which means I have to be task-oriented to avoid getting distracted.

The thing is, my mind can easily take an average day and thrust it into high drama. The mom me worries about my kids, the business me is obsessed about sales, and the chola puffs up at the thought of being disrespected. I'm not at war with these characters. They're my Locas. They're the paint colors in my vibrant life. But they're loud and can be overwhelming. And in addition to these characters' theatrical performances on any given day, there are the many distractions that have come to exist in my everyday life—like my cell phone, laptop, relationships, and Netflix.

It's a very noisy world. Taking the time to get quiet is a requirement for maintaining sanity.

The spiritual part of me craves quiet. She calls it inner peace. She sees the futility in all the fuss but needs the vehicle to take all the Locas for a ride to the beach.

**"MEDITATION IS NOT A WAY OF MAKING YOUR MIND QUIET. IT'S A WAY OF ENTERING INTO THE QUIET THAT'S ALREADY THERE—BURIED UNDER THE FIFTY THOUSAND THOUGHTS THE AVERAGE PERSON THINKS EVERY DAY."**

**- DEEPAK CHOPRA**

I found that meditation is another tool in my healing arsenal that has changed my life. I use meditation for so many things. I meditate to start my day with clarity or restore balance at the end of a crazy day. I also use it to improve productivity or creativity. Through meditation I've learned that I can easily tap into inner peace, focus, and tranquility anytime and anywhere I please.

I want to elaborate on what meditation feels like for me because truthfully, there was a point in my life when I had no frame of reference for the term "inner peace." I knew only what it meant to be in one place and, no matter what, feel like I wanted to be somewhere else. This was a state of disease, and although my body was young and healthy, my mind and spirit were discontented. Meditation allowed me to turn the volume down on life's chaos and tune in to the place inside me where there is so much joy that I can almost feel high. It's like having God's personal address and being able to drive there anytime. That may sound wacky to some people. But I don't care, because honestly, some of my meditative moments have been divine. And if I can encourage one person to begin this practice, I'll have succeeded in my mission.

Meditation doesn't have to be a big deal. Just get quiet enough to recognize your own thought patterns without judgement. From there, you can decide if and how you want to change those patterns. You can learn to use your meditation practice to achieve some fascinating results, but the most important thing is just to start somewhere. I did a lot of research on meditation. I read, watched videos, and took various classes. There's so much information out there that scientifically proves that meditation reduces stress and eases anxiety. We now know more than ever before about how meditation affects our minds and bodies. It's almost sad to think that, despite all this research, more isn't being done to teach meditation on a grander scale.

Meditation works for people of all ages, too. Years ago I got an email from my son's teacher. She mentioned that in order to provide a physical resource for managing academic stress, the students did a thirty-minute mindfulness activity, relaxing different parts of the body and creating a safe place within their minds that they could go to when needed. She said I should ask the kids about it. So I did. My kids were excited to share their safe spaces with me. And I was excited to find that I had a tool in my arsenal to help them cope with stress. If you have family members who struggle with mental health issues or addiction, you understand that healthy coping is a gift. Mindfulness has helped me cope and has been a total blessing in my life.

There are literally dozens of ways to meditate. There is the body scan, guided, mantra, and breath work, to name a few. One blogger suggested that any activity in which you can slow down your mind to become more inwardly focused and more rooted in the present moment can offer the benefits of meditation. His post Meditation Techniques for the Busy or Impatient is full of ideas for taking the pressure off meditating "correctly" and just reaping the benefits of slowing down:

1. Exercise meditation: Walking, running, swimming, biking, yoga, etc.
2. Bathing meditation: Turn your shower or bathtub into a spa experience.
3. Music meditation: Music is such a powerful tool. Set an intention for your next playlist.
4. Hobby meditation: Paint, write, color, garden—just BE free and allow your mind to fully focus.
5. Massage meditation: HELLO! I'm sure to incorporate this into a more regular practice because I just met the most special massage therapist on planet Earth.
6. If all else fails, he says: Try the ten-minute dark room meditation or five-minute dimly lit room meditation.

So now you know that there are many ways to meditate, and I hope you'll explore! I found that guided meditation was an easy way for me to start. Meditating on your own requires some effort, and it can be tough to meditate without a teacher or guide. Guided meditations literally walk you through the process and help you find a calm, peaceful state—one step at a time. I've recorded a basic five-minute meditation for anyone who wants to try it out or needs a quick tune-up! You can find it on YouTube.

While on the subject of quiet time, I have to mention sleep. Throughout my life I've had a love/hate relationship with sleep. From my teens until early on in my marriage, I struggled with bouts of insomnia. My mind would just get so hyper-focused on something that I couldn't go to sleep. I remember the day I was cured of this. To give you the full picture, I'll have to share about my brother Rick.

It would be hard to put into words the impact Rick had on me when he was alive. Maybe in some way I have deified him—which, of course, he would hate because Rick was painfully in touch with his imperfections.

Rick was seventeen years older than me and I only briefly remember him from my childhood. Many of those memories were not great because he was on drugs during the early years of my life. Anyone who has lived through addiction has a clear picture of what life looked like at the time of his using, but for those of you who don't, I'll elaborate a bit.

Throughout my childhood and adolescence, Rick experienced bouts of jail time, homelessness, and theft—even within the family. As a kid, I remember my mom warning me not to go with my brother no matter what. I must have been five at the time, and I was so wounded by this. My brother was outrageous and big and strong. I was so proud of him. He would come pick me up, take me to the park, and set up an impromptu comedy show in the street or on the train. I loved this more than anything because my job was simple: I was to laugh at the top of my lungs while he belted out, "Thank you very much! My name is Rick Aviles and you have just seen the debut of my little sister!" And that would be the beginning of his act. The act lasted only about fifteen minutes, but watching him was pure magic. He could take away his audience's worries, troubles, and fears and replace them with hysterical laughter.

Even as a child I could see how powerful that was. At the end of the show, I would pass the hat among our impromptu audience, and my brother and I would have what felt like an endless bounty of change. It was always enough for us to buy a meal at one of the many restaurants that he loved. I would order whatever I wanted, and he would have a tuna melt. He would give me fifty cents and tell me that I had earned it. Then he would take me home.

I would be on cloud nine for weeks after a day with him. I didn't know that the bounty we'd earned would last him only for a night. I didn't realize that his fix was his master. So when Mom declared I couldn't see him, I was confused. Why couldn't he come and pick me up? Why couldn't he be my rescuer? I imagine now that she was terrified for me, knowing what she did about her son. One day, mom and I were in the East Village, coming from a meal at our favorite Indian spot. We heard a loud familiar voice, ranting unintelligibly. It was Rick, and people were crossing the street to avoid him. As we got closer, he looked at us like we were familiar faces that he couldn't put his finger on. For a minute, he was still and quiet, but then quickly returned to yelling and bolting down the street. I was devastated. My brother was so sick, and I didn't know if I would ever see him again. Rick bounced in and out of rehab for most of my youth until one day it stuck and he remained clean until his death.

During his dope-fiend years, Rick had had many opportunities and burned many bridges. That's what happens when you're a slave to substance. Fortunately, his luck, talent, and relentless pursuit of a life in comedy allowed him to overcome the horrifying reputation he had created for himself. He became known as a talented and committed artist, landing larger parts on television and in film. Many people would recognize him from his roles in *Ghost, The Godfather Part III, and Carlito's Way.* Others remember Rick as the host of *Showtime at the Apollo* or his HBO episode of *One Night Stand.* He was doing the damn thing, but his was a story that ended too early.

He had already lived with HIV for years. I guess I knew he was sick, but I was a teen and in my own world. So it wasn't until I moved to Los Angeles that he became my best friend and mentor. His generosity was second to none and his hoarse voice was always so full of humor and honesty.

My own drinking and drugging had worn me out early, but at twenty-two, I got clean. Not having a buffer between the world and my feelings wasn't easy. Rick inspired me to live in my own rawness. How uncomfortable it was at first to face every aspect of life with no form of anesthetic, but I got used to it, sort of. It was always good to come home to him and make fun of the people we encountered. Rick could meet a person for five minutes and create a hilarious character around them. He was a master of dialects but also a master of observation. So many of the jokes he told were about himself. He was an ever-evolving emotional work in progress and I loved him with every fiber of my being.

Rick was my older brother, but I felt it my duty to keep him well. I shopped for him and cleaned his house. I stocked up on food and learned to cook so I could keep his weight up.

On top of having HIV, he was also a non-compliant diabetic. I would reprimand him when I found candy wrappers in his car, and he would joke that the doctor told him that it was okay. He would then add that he had also been informed that wine and heroin were allowed on his birthday. We would burst into laughter at his foolishness. We shared a dark sense of humor. Both of us knew that the candy wouldn't be the death of him. I know it seems naïve, but something in me truly believed that I could keep him alive until they found a cure. It wasn't until my second year in Los Angeles that Rick started to show real signs of sickness—at least that I was willing to see.

It was 1993. I was pregnant and he was on a medication that was pumped directly from a ball that he kept in his pocket to a catheter in his chest. I had no idea what all his medications were for, which only made me more aggressive in planning meals for him. I stopped in one day to deliver some food and check on him. I let myself in and found blood everywhere. A feeling of panic came over me. I called him, and in a faint voice he answered. I ran to his bedroom and found him slumped over in his chair, still naked from the shower with just a bloody towel loosely wrapped around him.

The area on his chest around the catheter was swollen and had become infected. In his pain and impatience, he had removed the needle. I took him to the hospital and waited for him. It was around that time that I became his next of kin. I was twenty-four, pregnant, and now responsible for my dying brother.

When I went back to his home, I cleaned up the blood and began to think that his life might be slipping away. I didn't for a minute think about my own safety—only that the medical industry had better be quick to find a cure because I wasn't ready to lose him.

I had to live walking distance from him, so we got him an apartment in our complex in Venice.

Eighteen months later, my brother became so weak that at

times he wasn't recognizable. But I refused to let up on his meal plan. It was my one hope. I must have seemed delusional.

At my daughter's first birthday party, Rick sat in the corner, watching the kids play. He didn't eat a crumb. I remember telling him that I would make something special for him to take home. He said, "Please don't, Sis. I can't eat." His words caused a pang in my stomach but I pushed past the emotion. I could see he was too weak to walk by himself, so I had Rico escort him home. Rick was to go into the hospital for a test of some kind in the next few days. I was sure that I would drop him off, they would help him, and he would be back to normal.

When I got the call from the hospital telling me he was gone, it was like God had taken a hammer to my head. That was the force I felt as I fell to the floor. My mom said that I screamed, but I don't remember screaming. I only remember thinking that I didn't know what to do with this kind of pain.

I went to the hospital to identify his body. He was in a room marked "Hazardous." The big, bold sign was there to warn all who were near that this thing was to be handled with caution. I was LIVID. My brother was not a thing. He was EVERYTHING. When I walked in, he was lying on the bed and I remember yelling for him to get up. My mom tried to calm me, but I was inconsolable. I shook him and screamed until she finally slapped me out of my hysteria. To this day, these moments stand out in my mind as the worst of my life.

I will probably have to write an entire book of stories about Rick, but this section is about rest. I gave you that insight so you could gauge the level of stress my mind and body were under. About a month after he died, I was a complete mess. I thank God that Rick had some incredible people in his life and that he was prepared to go with no loose ends, because I was useless. The devastation of his passing consumed me. You have to understand that in my life, he was truly one of the only men

I trusted. He was the only person I could be my whole self with and who just accepted me without any expectations.

My mom had moved to Los Angeles to help me with my daughter, as well as to help Rick. Rick and Mom had always had a strained relationship, but he let her be a nurturing mother to him at the end. He didn't guilt her for all the fucked-up things she had done as a young mom who hadn't known what to do with a son with ADD. At the end, he just let her be a mom. Some of you reading this will know what a gift that was to her. To be forgiven is a truly liberating thing. It allowed my mom to be a total fucking champion at the time. She buried her son and then watched her daughter slide into a state of depression that would have freaked many people out.

I was a new mom, barely eating or sleeping and in no condition to take care of a child. I would have moments of almost catatonic states accompanied by stomach pangs. My mom would often take my baby with her for the day. She hoped that I would rest, but I didn't. I would just clean or stare out the window.

One night, while I lay in bed and stared blankly at the ceiling, the pain in my gut was so severe that I contemplated making myself vomit to see if I might gain some relief. Suddenly, at the foot of my bed, sat my brother. I was surprised at first—elated, actually—but then I panicked! I knew he wasn't supposed to be there. Intuitively, he addressed my fear. He assured me that this was a much-needed visit on both parts. He needed me to be okay and he knew that I needed to know he was okay.

He spoke to me of an indescribable knowing, loving, and peace. He took me around the world and allowed me to see and feel what he felt as he traveled his new universe. I was so amazed by the intense fuchsia and gold elements everywhere. I later came to learn that the color fuchsia represents meditation and connection to spirituality—letting go of old attitudes and welcoming a new change. This color is also associated with emotional stability. The golden color reflects a spiritual reward, richness, refinement, and enhancement of surroundings. It also signifies determination and an unyielding nature.

I'm open-minded and the fact is I don't know if the spirit of my brother really visited me or if my exhausted brain came up with this dream as a way to preserve my life. What I DO know is that after the dream, I was able to function. Twenty years later I still miss my brother, my best friend, my mentor, my cheerleader, but I'm so grateful to have found relief from the kind of pain that could have literally killed me.

What made this moment a historic marker in my life? That was the moment I realized that I could survive anything and, more importantly, that I WANTED to.

I slept like a baby after Rick's visit.

Sleep is no joke when it comes to mental and physical wellness. I know the havoc lack of sleep can cause, so I don't mess around when it comes to getting enough rest. The National Sleep Foundation has this to say about catching your z's:

"The first thing experts will tell you about sleep is that there is no 'magic number.' Not only do different age groups need different amounts of sleep, but sleep needs are also individual. Just like any other characteristics you are born with, the amount of sleep you need to function best may be different for you than for someone who is of the same age and gender."

Okay, so chances are that between shopping, cooking, events, parties, heartbreak, sniffles, and other circumstances, you may not get as much sleep as you'd normally need. Enter the busy person's quick body repair shop: THE NAP.

I'm a fan of the nap. About three years ago, I gave up the guilt I felt about taking them. Contrary to popular opinion, napping isn't for the lazy or depressed. Famous nappers have included Bill Clinton, Lance Armstrong, Leonardo da Vinci, and Thomas Edison.

I don't know what it was about running myself ragged that made me feel like I was achieving something, but I had to stop. The first consideration was mindset: I recognized that I wasn't being lazy. Napping actually made me more productive, and I was more alert and cheerful after I woke up. It turns out scientific studies are showing how great naps are for people of all ages.

I find that as I get older, foods that are heavy in fat and sugar can really mess with my ability to fall asleep. Back in the day, my grandmother would make me a cup of warm (full-fat) milk right before bed. I would sleep like a baby. The trick is that milk and other dairy products contain an amino acid (which help induce sleep) known as tryptophan. Tryptophan is important for the production of serotonin in the body.

If you don't drink milk, there are plenty of other sources of tryptophan:

- Animal meat (chicken, turkey, red meat)
- Dairy products
- Eggs
- Soy
- Spirulina
- Seaweed
- Spinach
- Fish/seafood
- Pumpkin, sunflower seeds, and almonds
- Bananas
- Dates
- Legumes

My mom used to always say, "You snooze, you lose." But as it turns out, you snooze, you win! Give it a try for yourself and see if you aren't amazed at the results!

# Script Supervision

How to manifest goals using the power of words.

*A*s an actor, I read hundreds of screenplays. Screenplays are the foundation of a film. They're the words on a page that set the location and give life to the characters through dialogue. Screenplays are also called *playbooks* or *scripts*. If you're in healthcare, prescriptions (scripts for short) may also be a part of your everyday work life. The Merriam-Webster dictionary defines the word prescription as "the action of laying down authoritative rules or directions," as well as an "ancient or long-continued custom." Truth be told, we live in a world where scripts are written and executed at every moment.

Scripts are little programs, or codes, that breathe life into everything. From our cell phones to the streetlights in front of our homes, everything runs on a script. While we may be somewhat aware of the little programs that run our computers, the real trip is the script that runs in our head.

Remember the formulas I mentioned earlier? They're just tiny, over-simplified scripts that run in the subconscious mind. It seems that our subconscious mind has a book of scripts that runs pretty much everything in our lives.

Numerous studies have revealed that only 5 percent of our

cognitive activities (decisions, emotions, actions, behavior) are conscious. So the subconscious mind is the *mera mera* (*big boss*) in our head. All those scripts I referred to earlier were scripts written by a five-year-old girl trying to survive. God bless that baby, but she has no business running the entire life of a grown-ass businesswoman.

I want to explain that this is my belief system regarding the subconscious mind. If you're interested in psychology, you can read a plethora of material that will offer all kinds of theories about how this part of the brain works.

I call my subconscious mind Baby Gangsta, and I believe that her mission in life is to protect me. She always has my back physically. She's super-organized when it comes to bodily functions like breathing and keeping my immune system in shape. My girl is a bit of a gangster when it comes to protecting my emotions, though. You see, homegirl witnessed some things as a kid, and she's quick to get upset. Fortunately, she's smart. She learns by experience, and I've learned how to walk her through the tough scenarios that come up. This chapter is all about words and scripts and how I learned to slowly make edits to the many programs written by Baby Gangsta.

### "ONCE YOU CRACK THE SCRIPT, EVERYTHING ELSE FOLLOWS."

### – RIDLEY SCOTT

There are two word techniques I use to maintain and manifest in my life. Ready? I'm about to blow your mind here:

I write words. I speak words.

I know that sounds super simple, but I'm not going to leave you hanging. In this chapter I break down some specific ways of writing and speaking that I use. I hope that by implementing these simple techniques, you too will find some relief from the gangsta running your mind.

Over the years, people would ask me when I was going to write a book. I would say, "One day," but the truth is, I didn't know how I was going to do it or what I would say. For one thing, I've always loved books, but I didn't enjoy writing. The power of writing, indeed, came as a surprise to me. And I'm so grateful it did.

In a previous chapter I shared with you how one of the most, if not THE most, potent insights came to me in the form of a loving letter of forgiveness. It's almost crazy to think that a cluster of words scribbled on a page can lead to one of the most profound moments of awakening, but it's true.

I'm an extremely sensitive creative whose mind can quickly get cluttered. In my head I keep track of who hurt me and how I'll get them later. I could blame that craziness on being a Scorpio or being Latina, but really, those are just excuses.

It's actually Baby Gangsta! She's a militant scorekeeper who shows up and watches all things rigorously. Even though I've learned that I can't be that person and live my best life at the same time, random stuff will just come up to distract me. In addition to that mess in my head are also the schedules I have to keep, goals I want to attain, and brilliant thoughts I want to share. I can easily get overwhelmed by all this.

## The Written Word

I use the written word to clean up my mind space. And I'm not talking about books. I'm talking about journals.

At the time I wrote my forgiveness list, I had begun working with a couple of coaches who provided insight to some real breakthroughs. Other wisdom came from books and online courses I was taking. It was the first time that I remember questioning the things I believed about myself. It was also my first foray into permitting myself to change those beliefs. I had so many questions and was learning so much. Note-taking became a part of my everyday life, and I wrote several journals at that time. This book includes pieces from my journal writing.

As you've now read, my state of being when I started journaling was erratic. I was suffering on a personal level and in a career rut. Good things still came from that time of desperation, though. For one, I opened myself up to the sages who were put on my path. When you're humble enough to ask for help, life has a funny way of giving you what you need.

Some of my ideas came from areas deep in my subconscious, and some were surface ideas that casually supported those beliefs. It was a lot of information to sort through. To preserve what little sanity I seemed to have left, I had to find a place outside my head to do the sorting. I thank God for paper and pen, as well as for Google Docs!

Most of us have either had our own or heard about someone who has had a diary or journal, right? Did you know that therapists and counselors widely recommend journaling as a tool to supplement therapy? I've read that people who consistently journal report understanding themselves better, staying more in touch with feelings, and being better able to deal with the past.

I highly recommend journaling. You can call your mental dumping ground a journal, a diary, a notebook, or whatever you want. If you're like me, just writing things down is a life-saving tool. Each style of writing has had a place in my healing.

Back in the day, stores used to be jammed with items to market to little girls. I remember all these cute diaries that had locks so we could keep our secrets safe. The first diary I remember having was when I was in fourth grade. The cover was this intricately embellished Asian print. I remember recording the events of the days spent with Mom. I had just been reunited with her after years of living with my dad. Our time together was still a novelty.

I also remember journaling as a teen. In those years, in addition to recording events, I wrote down thoughts, poems, and song lyrics. I even developed some codes for my journal— symbols that stood for things like smoking weed or hanging out with a particular person. I saved several of my diaries into my young adulthood but got rid of them when I got more "serious" about life. Later on I threw out the thoughts and dreams of teen Angel too. She was a silly party girl who dreamed of moving to Hollywood. I had already been there and done that. This newer version of me was a mom. I was busy and had little time to indulge in the fantastic ideas of a young artist. Frankly, the mom version of me was embarrassed by and a little afraid of her teenage self.

It's almost backward to think that as we get busier with life, we ditch journals. But that's what I did. Having a place to record dreams, organize thoughts, or let out fears should be a priority. I didn't realize it, but giving up journaling was just another example of how I allowed my creativity to be devalued.

In my twenties I moved into my Franklin Planner stage, when I would record the plans for the day. My sister gifted me my first planner. Sis is by far the most traditionally successful person in my family. She's a super type-A personality who's the queen of manifestation and planning. When she gave me that first book, I took it to heart not only because she had her shit together but because I knew she wanted the best for me. I knew she wasn't giving me just a book, but also a key. Each page was lined, and every minute could be blocked out and accounted for. This may seem super rigid to some, but when I went back to school, this planner saved my ass. As a mom with a young child, a home to keep up, and school to attend, there was no way for me to do it all without writing things down. To this day I keep a planner like this, and it's the best tool I know for goal-setting.

Now, this is where we recognize our role as the scriptwriters and supervisors of our own lives, and we do something about it. The scriptwriter is a creator, and the supervisor is the executor. You need both.

As the writer, you have the chance to indulge yourself in purging distraction or creating a fantastic world.

As the supervisor, you're responsible for the continuity. On a film set, the supervisor saves the director's ass by focusing on the tiny details. Have you ever seen a movie where an actor has one hairstyle, shirt, prop, or makeup look in one scene, but then something different in another? They had no script supervisor! And guess what? It's the notes taken by the script supervisor during the shooting of a scene that help everyone, including the editor cutting the movie.

Statistics show that people who write down their goals are more than 80 percent more likely to achieve them. So from the more serious business perspective of things, a goal that's written down is more likely to get done.

To this day, my planner is an essential part of my life. I still feel a certain degree of satisfaction from checking off the items that I was able to get done over the day.

The power of writing can be helpful in all aspects of life. Whether real-life rantings, class note-taking, doodling, or dream recording, I've gotten great relief from keeping a journal. But not all journals are the same. I'm going to cover several types of techniques that I've used and how they served my needs. I have them categorized in two types: clean-up and storytelling.

Where you begin is up to you, but I began with cleaning up.

## Morning Pages

I started by using the morning pages technique from Julia Cameron's book *The Artist's Way*. I highly recommend this book to everyone. Morning pages are three pages of handwritten, stream-of-consciousness writing that you do first thing in the morning. They're not high art. As a matter of fact, they're not even writing.

Morning pages can provoke, clarify, comfort, cajole, and help you prioritize and synchronize the day. But for me, morning pages freed up space in my head and had a profound effect on me. I still have my morning pages journals in a storage bin inside my closet. I went back to them for reference for this book, but they're just pages and pages of ramblings.

For me, the morning pages weren't a recording of events; they were just a safe space for me to let out all my thoughts and feelings onto paper. These journals served as a blubbering confessional where I could just pour out the good, the bad, and the ugly, and cleanse my thoughts of judgment.

## A Brain Dump

I was surprised at what a relief it was to just pour it all out. In more recent years, I've seen a version of this style of journal-keeping called a brain dump.

A brain dump is basically when you dump all the contents of your mind onto paper or a digital document. It's kind of like what you would do if you were cleaning out a drawer or purse. But as in dumping out a bag or drawer, the intention is to eventually organize. With that being said, the difference between morning pages and a brain dump is intention. Morning pages were more of a cleanser for me, and the brain dump was a tidying-up or organizational tool.

Go ahead and try brain dumping here or use your journal.

So aside from cleaning and organizing, how can writing help us manifest our desires? Both dumps and pages work for me at different times, but an essential addition to my writing is focused on intentional positivity. Here are some techniques I've discovered to use writing to change lives.

## The Curated List

From my forgiveness letter, you can probably tell that I'm a fan of lists. This was the first form of organization that my mama taught me. I love curated lists. I have gratitude lists, to-do lists, the occasional shopping list, but by far my favorite came to me one morning while lying in bed. I began to think of the many beautiful things in my life. I hate clutter, but I'm a DAILY collector of beautiful things. I curate and collect sensual moments; you know—the kind of things that pass but somehow magically show up in different ways.

Here's just a sample of what's on my list:

All kinds of kisses

The written, spoken, or gestured words "I love you"

Feeling beautiful without the need for confirmation

Hugs that end but that you wish wouldn't

The smell of dewy grass, eucalyptus, or pine at sunrise

Sunsets over the ocean

The face of a child understanding something they previously felt was impossible to learn

The feeling of a warm fire, radiator, blanket, or body on a cold night

The appearance of a loved one when I haven't seen them in ages

Clean water when I'm thirsty

Blooming flowers

The taste of fruit, heavy with ripeness and just off the tree

The gratitude of being able to offer hospitality and the warmth of being its recipient

The mist of warm water waves

Music that makes me cry, sing, or dance

Holding hands

Tickles and back scratches

The laughter that's so deep, parts of the body start to hurt or tears begin to fall

Looking around and seeing people of all colors, sizes, and shapes and knowing that they're family

Conversations that inspire thought

Extraordinary quiet

Being in the moment

I've had coaching clients do this assignment for thirty days straight. Every single one has given me great feedback. So if you want to raise your vibe in thirty days, try the curated list technique. Try to add to your list daily without repeats.

## Affirmations

You can write affirmations for anything you'd like to manifest. I've used this technique multiple times, and it works! An affirmation is a declaration that something is real. Transforming your life through affirmative scripting is possible but may require a bit of work.

Some of you struggle with the negative things you've been programmed to believe. Writing statements without feeling good will do little to change your life. Thoughts evoke feelings, and then those feelings power additional thoughts, actions, and results. Without feeling good, you might just as well do nothing.

You may struggle with affirmations because you feel fake. There is HOPE for you.

When writing an affirmation, avoid using negative language. Write your affirmation in the positive "I AM" format. If you no longer want to be angry, write "I AM cheerful, happy, and pleased!" instead of "I AM not angry." Or at least write "I AM free from anger."

## Future-Self Love letters

If you can't arrive at your affirmations from a TRUE place, try writing a letter to yourself from the future.

Tell yourself where you are and remind yourself that the limitations you placed on yourself were temporary. I can't express enough how effective this technique can be in relieving anxiety. No matter what you're dealing with, from lovesickness to bankruptcy, realize that your future self has already overcome. Your future self lives in the place of your dreams and is unlimited, wise, and at peace. Feel free to ask questions or even ask your future self to write your affirmations!

## Notes to God or the Universe

Some people have written letters to the Universe and witnessed incredible success. I haven't tried this technique, but it's something that I believe would be a powerful tool for someone who's spiritually inclined.

Decide on the purpose of your letter and get to writing. Do you need to forgive or want forgiveness? Ask. Do you know precisely what you want to see in your life, or do you need clarity? Ask. Your letter to God can be a printed version of a prayer. You can literally make it about anything you want or need.

## The Empowering Inquisition

Be open and keep an ongoing list of questions that you phrase in a way that emphasizes positivity and steers you in the direction of your goals.

Here was my first empowering inquisition list:

How can I be so happy?

What can I do RIGHT now that will make me smile?

Why does God love me so much?

Where did I learn how to forgive like a champion?

How did I get to be so smart?

How did I raise my kids to be so well adjusted?

Why do people at my job respect me so much?

How did I get so lucky?

Where did all this extra money come from?

When am I going to stop being such an amazing mom?

Why does it feel so good to buy beautiful things for myself?

How did I get so confident and comfortable with myself?

What are my favorite things about myself?

Why do things always work out for the best?

How did I suddenly stop giving more credit to what other people thought and start valuing myself?

Why is it okay to be beautiful and smart?

Why do I love what I do so much?

How can life get even better?

What do I look forward to?

Why am I so blessed?

How did I get so powerful?

When did I stop fearing men?

How can I teach other women what I know?

## The Character Description

A good character description tells as much about the narrator as it does about the character. It's the narrator, after all, who's observing the character.

So as you write about yourself, write in a way that shows your kindness and admiration for yourself. Observe what you love about yourself in the future. This was another exercise I did very early on in my journey.

Here's my description of SHE. "She" was the me I wanted to be. She was not who I felt I was then, but who I aspired to be. I'm happy to say that this is the me I am today. I LOVE a good story, but I didn't know how essential a story would be to the transformation of my own life.

*SHE*

*When she walks into the room, she has the "X" factor. What IS the "X" factor? It's more than beauty or sex. It's what the French say is je ne sais quois (something that cannot be adequately described or expressed). "X" looks like confidence, not arrogance. It's easy for her to be in her skin. She likes being in it. She's in control. She's funny. Smart. She has her own sense of style. She doesn't care what's "in" because she knows what looks good on her. She likes the way she smells: Sometimes it's like tangy citrus, sometimes like exotic spices from the East. She enjoys being different. She loves and accepts her own versatility. She's like a chameleon. She can be tough. She can be gentle. She's unafraid to embrace ALL that she is. She's proud of all that she's become as a result of her life experience. She's open. She shares her experiences, her thoughts, and her feelings. She doesn't fear judgment from others. What can man do to her? She's confident in her relationship with God and the Universe. She's a student soaking up everything she can to grow into a more incredible and complete person. She's a mom. She loves her kids and teaches them how to balance loving themselves and others. She teaches them mindfulness and compassion. She's affectionate. She's passionate. She's confident in her sexuality. She accepts compliments; she doesn't dissect them but simply says "thank you" and lets them sink in. She can cleanse herself of negativity. She's a healer (an energy worker) first for herself, then for others. She loves her body. She makes sure to feed it healthy foods and lots of water, and she gets plenty of fresh air and exercise. She meditates daily to decrease stress and increase productivity. She stands tall. She speaks positively about herself and her situations.*

There's no right journaling style, just the right timing for each individual. Have you noticed the bullet journal craze these days? I love it. It can be time consuming, but I enjoy it in bite-sized doses. Find YOUR STYLE! Don't be afraid to have fun with your journals and planners. Also, get creative.

For instance you can:

1. Use both hands. When we write something with a pen or pencil, we instinctively perform this task with our dominant hand. But did you know you stimulate both sides of your brain when you write with both hands?
2. Write several sets. An example of a set is 3-3-3, which means you write an affirmation nine times: three times with your dominant hand, three times with your non-dominant hand, and three more times with your dominant hand.
3. Write in different ways: long hand, other languages you speak, all caps, script, typed, etc.
4. The more fun you make it, the more you'll want to do it.

Use the space here or use a journal to pick one of the six techniques I've listed to try right now.

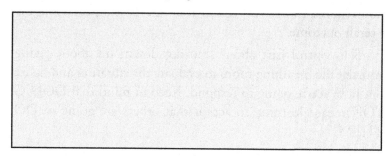

## The Spoken Word

I think as book readers, we all understand how important words can be. As in the written section, we must begin with the clean-up.

When it comes to speaking, it's all about self-control. Trash-talking is literally the junk food of the soul, so be mindful of the words you use to speak over yourself and others. Here's some simple advice from Disney: "If you can't say something nice, don't say anything at all." Avoid lies, avoid arguing to prove a point. Sometimes silence is truly golden.

This may feel like it goes against your policy of keeping it real. Trust me when I tell you that Baby Gangsta has all kinds of shit to say. But if you're on a mission to keep it real, you've got to go into the core of who you are. Once you're there, you can determine what's actually real, and what you want to change.

If you're in a toxic environment, the most productive thing you can do is figure out a way to get out. If you're hurt by or feel disrespected by someone you care for, learning to effectively communicate will be the best chance you have of saving that relationship. I have struggled with this so many times. I've used words with the intention of hurting someone else because I wanted them to feel as bad as I did. In most cases, no matter how relieved I was to express myself, I never felt great about the overall outcome.

Self-control isn't about shutting down. It's about giving yourself the breathing room to evaluate the situation and figure out how you're going to respond. Keep in mind that DOING YOU means learning to accept that others are going to DO THEM.

Self-control is also not something reserved for your communication with others. When it comes to self-talk, recognize that it's not okay to put yourself down. If you're always talking about how dumb, broke, ugly, and not enough you are, stop that shit. If you've been told those things, for starters, I want to tell you that I'm sorry. No one should be spoken to in that way. But now that you're on a journey of self-care and appreciation, you can do better.

A lot of times we talk shit about ourselves in a joking manner. Self-deprecating humor is a sign of modesty. It's a way that comedians and people in leadership positions put others at ease. But this is a tricky space to play in. Because, while we want to project to others that we don't take ourselves too seriously, we also have to watch how much of this type of humor we use. Self-deprecation can backfire. Other people might actually start believing you, but most importantly, Baby Gangsta might start believing you, too. She'll hold you to what you say about yourself. So be wise.

Once you've conditioned yourself to stop negative language, train yourself to say lovely things:

## I'M WORTHY OF ABUNDANCE.
## I'M BEAUTIFUL.
## I'M CREATED IN GOD'S IMAGE.
## I DESERVE GOOD.
## I ACCEPT LOVE AND JOY.
## I AM LOVE. I AM JOY!

I love words, and I believe they're tools of power. Some of the most profound experiences of my life have happened because of words. I've heard words that have hurt more than childbirth. I've also heard phrases that felt better than a massage. I've read that words are manifesting commands to the subconscious mind.

So, when we speak words out loud, we're actually telling Baby Gangsta to make it happen. Understanding how exactly this occurs probably calls for a course of study in brain science as well as philosophy. And it may never be fully understood. But humankind has always been fascinated by this form of communication.

Here are some provocative thoughts and quotes to consider:

## "LIFE AND DEATH ARE IN THE POWER OF THE TONGUE ..."

## - PROVERBS 18:21

## "ALL THAT WE ARE IS THE RESULT OF WHAT WE HAVE THOUGHT. IF A MAN SPEAKS OR ACTS WITH AN EVIL THOUGHT, PAIN FOLLOWS HIM. IF A MAN SPEAKS OR ACTS WITH A PURE THOUGHT, HAPPINESS FOLLOWS HIM, LIKE A SHADOW THAT NEVER LEAVES HIM."

## - BUDDHA

## "WHEN YOU HAVE SPOKEN THE WORD, IT REIGNS OVER YOU. WHEN IT IS UNSPOKEN, YOU PREVAIL OVER IT."

## - ARABIAN PROVERB

Did you know?

Every letter in the Hebrew alphabet has a design, a number, and a meaning.

It's believed that in Sanskrit, each syllable has an effect on the body.

In Hawaiian shamanism, there's a source of power behind the words of the language. The ancient Hawaiians acknowledged the spiritual, divine meaning behind the sounds and tones that make up the words.

Regardless of the belief system, most people will agree that words are powerful. I composed a short list of my favorite words. Whether the positive feeling I get from hearing these words comes from the word itself or from the meaning I've assigned isn't essential to me. What matters is that I use these words in affirmations about myself and others:

How awesome it is that I can write and share the words on my mind freely! There are people all over the world who can't. Words can motivate, inspire, and change. I try to speak my favorite words, or variations of them, in some form EVERY DAY.

Kind words feel good. Do you speak words of power over yourself and your loved ones? What words make the top of your list? If you don't yet have a practice of speaking life over others, try it. Have fun. Be bold. Share your victories with people who deserve your trust!

You're creating a life with words. Remember to be the script supervisor and keep yourself and Baby Gangsta on track.

# Catching Your Breath

## Conscious breathing creates a connection to self.

AVE YOU EVER had a panic or anxiety attack? I have, and let me tell you, it's not fun. If you've never had one but someone described one to you, it's probably ten times more horrifying than they were even able to express.

My attacks always felt like they started as a heightened sense of awareness and ended in my chest. The start of the attack might be a fleeting thought like, *I'm going to be trapped in here.* Or the beginning could be a sudden awareness of the hair raising on the back of my neck. In other words, out of nowhere—fear. Then, I would suddenly feel like I couldn't breathe and anxiety would set in. Trust me when I tell you, I know that I can be dramatic, but I'm not exaggerating when I say that the fear of a panic attack can feel like death knocking.

The Mayo Clinic says symptoms of panic disorder often start in the late teens or early adulthood and affect more women than men. Now, here's the trip: The Mayo Clinic also has a list of factors that may increase the risk of developing panic attacks or panic disorder. On that list are some things that I'll never know about, like "family history of panic attacks or panic disorder." In my family, there was no time for anxiety or panic.

My mom's side of the family seemed to be built out of rock.

Despite rickets, rigorous plantation work, a botched C-section, and an abandoned marriage, my maternal grandmother, Nana, was a small-framed bundle of spiritual joy and physical wellness. My mom, though not nearly as healthy as Nana, had the advantage of her education. My mom used the tools at her disposal to manage her stress. Carmen could also blow a gasket and cuss someone out, but anxiety and panic attacks weren't a part of her repertoire.

That would leave me to guess that if my panic attacks were genetic, they would have had to have come from my dad's side. My paternal grandmother had a host of illnesses. When I was a child, my opinion of her was that she was as mean as a snake. Looking back on her life now, I view it with much more empathy. Doña Paca was non-English speaking Puerto Rican who had been transplanted from her warm Caribe home to the cold and sometimes dangerous South Bronx. Most people in my family would probably say Doña Paca was a hypochondriac. She certainly had the pills to support that assessment, but maybe what she really had was panic disorder.

Who even knows what she left behind on that island. Was there abuse? Hunger? Shame? Maybe the better life in America that her husband had promised didn't end up panning out like she thought it would.

The Mayo Clinic also says that a traumatic event, such as sexual assault or a severe accident, can trigger panic disorder. Doña Paca had survived breast cancer. I remember the giant scars on her chest from her double mastectomy. Cancer and the removal of both breasts definitely qualify as a traumatic event in my book.

As far as my own battle with panic, there are two huge red flags on that Mayo Clinic list. Number one is "major life stress, such as the death or serious illness of a loved one." My first panic attack showed up three years after my mom died.

Coincidence? Maybe. But when I read number two, "history of childhood physical or sexual abuse," Then I knew it wasn't a coincidence. It had to be Baby Gangsta!

Really? Yes. Trauma from any kind of abuse can rear its ugly head many times throughout a person's life. I wanted to think that I got the help I needed. But the truth is that sometimes things can resprout. To be clear, I happen to believe that resprouting is different from harping on things. When I first sought help to deal with the molestation, I did some work. I didn't share it with my mom or too many other people. I established my first layer of forgiveness, faced some of the ugly, and made a sort of peace with it.

But these kinds of experiences are complicated. The scripts and codes were written. My emotions were all twisted up into this intricate knot of ideas that I identified as me. I told myself to get over it. I wanted to be over it. I didn't understand that years later, something could come up out of my life and practically strangle me. But sometimes the only way to get over something is to go right through it.

Sometimes people will dismiss panic, anxiety, or depression as "just being in your head." I seemed to attract that sort of person for a while. You may know the type who dismisses what they don't understand as crazy, silly, or nonsensical. It made things so much worse because, in addition to the actual panic attack, I had to carry the extra burden of embarrassment. I began judging my inability to manage my anxiety as a weakness. The last thing a sick person needs is to feel judged.

This is where forgiveness work really matters. If you suffer from any of the afflictions mentioned above, do yourself a favor and forgive yourself. Then forgive the people around you for not being able to help you. Chances are that they don't have first-hand experience with your condition. And in all fairness to all of you, how can you expect someone to help you if they don't have a frame of reference?

For my own sanity, I had to deconstruct the idea that anxiety attacks were only in my mind or a sign of mental weakness. When I looked into the many reasons panic attacks occur, I discovered that they are both in the mind and body. If you suffer from symptoms of panic, go see a doctor and rule out certain medical conditions or other physical causes. If you've experienced long-term panic or anxiety, there's no shame in seeking out a mental health professional. Keep in mind that all professionals are not equal, so if you're not feeling someone, find someone new.

My advice: Be patient. Don't stop learning about yourself and don't let someone convince you to do something you don't feel good about. In addition to hiring someone who can help you sort out some of the things that are happening in your mind, the best gift you can give yourself is to learn how to master the functions of your body and mind.

I broke my left foot many years ago and developed arthritis. Years later I developed plantar fasciitis on that same foot. Some people might consider me unlucky. Some might say I was just experiencing normal wear and tear, and maybe it's true. But of course, I wanted to go a bit deeper. A friend referred me to a book by a woman named Louise Hay. It's called *You Can Heal Your Life*. In this book the author talks about the possible mental and emotional connections to physical conditions. In her book, Louise Hay states that foot problems indicate fear of the future and of not stepping forward in life.

This book is neither scientific nor based on medical research of any kind. Nevertheless, something amazing happened to me when I read it. I developed a more profound compassion for myself. I started to look more and more into the body/mind connection.

I learned about a theory that states problems on the left side of the body refer to an inability to ask for help, to receive, to surrender, and to be creative and trust our own wisdom. This resonated with me at my core. Could all this metaphysical information have a connection to psychology or even medicine? I could dismiss the repeated afflictions to my left foot as a coincidence. Or I could take a chance and believe that the pain was communicating to me that I needed some intentional self-care.

Once again, the signs pointed to Baby Gangsta, my purpose-filled subconscious mind. So much of my wellness journey addressed what I consider the trifecta of me: my body, mind, and spirit. For me to live my best life, the trifecta must operate optimally and together.

I take a holistic approach to whole-person wellness. If I'm struggling, I'm not afraid to look for help from multiple sources. I've seen doctors, therapists, ministers, coaches, and nutritionists—but most importantly, I train myself to listen to myself. For me, the most basic level of control over the physical body is awareness. And the most elemental physical process of the human body is breath. Proper breathing can change your life, and this goes for those of you who have no experience with panic, anxiety, or depression, too.

## "I TOOK A DEEP BREATH AND LISTENED TO THE OLD BRAG OF MY HEART. I AM, I AM, I AM."

### – SYLVIA PLATH, THE BELL JAR

So why have I dedicated a whole chapter to breathing?

Probably because breathing is life. Breathing properly brings more oxygen to the blood and the brain. There's no such thing as learning to breathe well. Once we take that first one in, most of us quickly become masters of breath. Sadly, for a variety of reasons, during our lives we start unlearning the natural flow of inspiration. We begin to forget the basics.

Tons of studies have looked at breathing. This book is not about psychology or science. It's about shifting beliefs. If you ever questioned what a fantastic being you are, think about this: As a human, you can consciously use breathing to influence your nervous system. Your nervous system regulates blood pressure, heart rate, circulation, digestion, and many other bodily functions.

I'm not going to say that if you master your breath, you'll cure all that ails you, but I am going to tell you that when it comes to life-changing techniques, breathing is a fucking beast.

During my panic attacks, I had to learn how to consciously (voluntarily) breathe so I wouldn't lose consciousness. But I need to emphasize that during a panic attack is not the time to learn technique. As a matter of fact, for me the worst time to learn anything was during a panic attack. I was so scared, critical, angry, and overwhelmed with emotion that simply remembering to breathe was all I could manage.

I had to practice breathwork daily to make my way through the panic and then to ultimately avoid it.

Maybe you don't have anxiety, but whatever your condition, learning proper breathing is one of the best things you can do for your physical and emotional health. Breath is a stabilizer for my emotional wellness. Have you ever noticed that the first thing someone trying to get another person out of a highly charged emotional situation says is, "Just breathe"?

We can look to science for proof of how our breath changes at different stages of emotion. Anger can be associated with shallow inhalations, forceful exhalations, and tension in the body.

In contrast, love, compassion, kindness, and wonder are related to deep, expansive, comfortable breathing. Restrictive breathing patterns also support the subconscious defense mechanisms behind stuffing or holding back unpleasant emotions. The truth is that I was full of anger and dealing with a lot of emotional baggage. Through panic attacks, my body was giving me some straight-up signs that it was time to deal with some long put-off issues.

There are many ways that you can learn how to breathe. You can go to YouTube, take a course at a community college, or try private yoga and meditation classes. If you'd rather die than sit in a class, I get it. Some of us had such shitty school experiences that the very idea of it may be a panic trigger in and of itself. Fortunately for you, there's another way for you to start your journey into breath. And it's hilarious!

As some of you may know, I come from a family of funny people. I don't just mean people with a sense of humor, but people who have made a living making other people laugh. After my brother Rick died, we had a memorial at the Laugh Factory in Hollywood. Rick Aviles was probably best known for his menacing role in *Ghost*, but he started his career as a stand-up comic. He was one of the first street comics. In the eighties, if you were lucky you might have caught him on the subway in New York City. While many people would think a comedy show as a memorial service is weird, this was Rick's wish. He wanted everyone to leave his funeral in tears ... of LAUGHTER.

Rick knew that laughter was the best medicine. I know this is true because, when I feel less than perfect, I like to call one particular friend who makes me cry out loud with laughter. This friend has the kind of laugh that's infectious. When she laughs, I don't even need to find what she said funny. I just start laughing, too. Inevitably, when I get off the phone, I feel better!

Of course, I did some research to find out why.

Laughing releases "happy chemicals" into the body. By letting laughter into every part of the body and mind, we chemically alter our physical state. And we immediately return to the here and now mentally. It's a physiological response.

If you're feeling less than 100 percent, try a little laugh therapy (also called laughing meditation or laughter yoga). The techniques simply involve inhaling deeply, then exhaling while laughing.

The next time you're alone, let yourself experience the freedom of spontaneous laughter. Don't worry if it feels weird at first. Give yourself permission to be quirky. Just laugh. No jokes, just giggle out of nowhere, like children do! One study on the subject stated that children laugh about four hundred to five hundred times a day, while an adult may laugh just fifteen times a day.

Why do kids get to laugh "just because," but adults determine that it's not okay for themselves? Jesus Christ, one of the greatest ascended masters of all time, said, "Truly I tell you, anyone who will not receive the kingdom of God like a little child will never enter it."

Spirituality and wellness can be peaceful, meditative, and quiet, but it can also be fun, silly, and amazing. Proper, deep meditative breathing, as well as laughter, have a special place in my wellness journey.

Just breathe. When you do what it takes to make deep breathing a part of your everyday practice, you indulge in the greatest gift you can give your own body, mind, and spirit.

I'm not a doctor, a therapist, or a religious leader. I'm simply a woman who went on a quest to cope with anxiety and find joy. Mission accomplished. What I came to believe and accept as real became the foundation of how I started to coach my clients. And now, the principles live in this book.

So let's get started on an exercise, shall we? I call this exercise the inspired body scan and I use it to begin my workshops.

Breathing has two phases, inspiration and expiration. I try to focus on the parts of my body that need a bit of extra help. I send inspired thoughts to those areas and let the negative thoughts expire.

Start by sitting or lying comfortably. The ideal position is sitting upright in an office or dining chair where you can put your feet flat on the floor. Put your hands, palms up, on your knees or thighs, and relax your back. If you're lying down, relax into the surface you're on.

Close your eyes and breathe slowly in through your nose. As you do this, imagine sending light, love, and oxygen down through your body. Send that breath to the very tips of your toes. As you breathe out through your mouth, collect any stress or tension in your body and let it out with the carbon dioxide.

Repeat this process, taking the breathwork up your body, from your feet, up to your legs, hips, buttocks, internal organs, ribs, chest, shoulders, arms, fingers, neck, face, and scalp. Really listen to your body. Are there areas that you feel are a bit more tense? Are you in pain? Spend a little more time in those areas. With each breath, send pure, clean, healing energy.

I love this body scan breathwork because it demands that I be in conscious contact with my body. It also requires me to be patient since I no longer rush past the parts of me that are in need. So many of us can go a lifetime without giving ourselves the luxury of breathing deeply into our own body. It's no wonder there's so much suffering when something so basic is ignored.

Now that you're breathing, I want you to start coming to

your senses. Focusing on the breath allows you to calm down enough to begin to focus on your senses.

After being in a dark place that I thought I could never return from, I was willing to try anything. For years I studied, prayed, meditated, and used the stimulation of my senses to bring me into balance. A lot of my healing has come from my awareness of energy.

# Coming To Your Senses

## How to enjoy living in the moment.

WHEN I FIRST started writing, I figured I would just create a workbook. You know, a few activities here and there. But as I started writing, I realized that you can find the exercises anywhere. The things I wanted to share were more intimate than instructions on breathing or meditation or any of the other tools you could find in other books. I wanted to share stories from my life. And I wanted to give you some insight into how my mind works. Or, more accurately, how I make peace with how it works!

Since Baby Gangsta has a large and comfy home inside my head, that's where I started to investigate. What I learned is that the *jefita*, or *boss babe*, running the me show, is a three-pound chunk of flesh called the brain. The brain is often described as a complex, electrically driven organ that works like a powerful computer. Still, from what I've read, it's much more than that. I've all but fallen in love with all the shit that it can do.

There's so much to know, and yet so little actually known about this fascinating part of us. I came to understand that with the brain, we create our own realities on every level— emotional, physical, and otherwise. The brain is responsible for perceiving data by reacting to a selected range of wavelengths, vibrations, or other stimuli. The selection of range is limited by a few factors: our genes, our past experiences, and our current state of attention. The current state of attention is where I started working my mindful practice.

To go from the grips of anxiety, panic attacks, and depression to where I am today is a miracle. This chapter is all about a process that helped me beyond what I could probably ever fully express.

When I started my journey, I just called this process "coming to my senses." I've since learned that what I learned to practice during this time is known as mindfulness. Mindfulness is often linked to meditation, which was also an essential element on my path to wellness. Mindfulness is actually just a state achieved by focusing awareness on the present moment. For some of you, this may seem too simple. I get it. I remember feeling that where I was, was the source of my anxiety. How could I possibly find peace from being in the moment if all I wanted to do was get out of it? If you're in that spot, I hope you choose to believe me when I tell you that transformation can happen in the exact place you are. And the result of that transformation can be anything you set your intention to be.

Baby Gangsta already had the basics of staying alive covered. But I wanted and needed more! I wanted to live and feel good, too. So I had to figure out how to ease stress and put pleasure into Baby Gangsta's agenda as well.

I began to look at the functions of my body, mind, and spirit in entirely new ways. I became more aware that everything within and around me has a range of vibrations. As I write this, I wonder how many of you will think I sound like a hippie, talking about vibes and shit. The reality is that vibrations are how we experience our senses. When I started engaging my brain on this level, I learned how to alter vibes and raise my consciousness in the process. More and more, I started testing out various ways to stimulate my brain by keeping my life full of stimuli that I loved.

Part of this was recognizing what felt right and then consciously recording that feeling. This required taking time for me. On walks I would pay full attention to what was around me, making sure to notice people hugging, the feeling of the Southern California sun on my arms, or the smell of flowers as I passed a local shop. I began to focus on the sounds of babies laughing or birds singing. I made sure that my phone wasn't on while I went on my sensory journeys because I didn't want to miss my real life while paying attention to a virtual one.

**"TO BE SENSUAL, I THINK, IS TO RESPECT AND REJOICE IN THE FORCE OF LIFE, OF LIFE ITSELF, AND TO BE PRESENT IN ALL THAT ONE DOES, FROM THE EFFORT OF LOVING TO THE BREAKING OF BREAD."**

**– JAMES BALDWIN, THE FIRE NEXT TIME**

## Sound

So, here we go. Our journey into this area will start with the most elemental state of vibration: sound. The most basic definition of sound is the transmitted vibrations of any frequency. It's hard to put into words what sound feels like, but I'll do my best by sharing a little story with you.

A few years ago, when my daughter was about seven, we were cleaning the house. I decided to YouTube a classical playlist. "Moonlight Sonata" by Beethoven came on.

Our conversation was as follows:

"Mom?" said my daughter.

"Yes, baby?"

"Is this Beethoven?"

"Yes, baby."

"We learned about him in school. He was deaf, huh?"

"Yes, he was."

"He could FEEL his music vibrations, huh?"

"Yes, he could."

"Well," she said with tears in her eyes, "I FEEL this."

A song that inspires tears of joy? DIVINE. Oh, how Beethoven knew this. He takes us on a journey of emotion in his three movements. And to understand that his tools for translating sound were not functioning correctly reinforces the concept of vibration. He felt his music, but where? In his soul? On his skin? In his brain? All of the above?

Sound is vibration. Our whole body absorbs and emits sound, and it has an optimum vibration. Even emotions and mental states have specific vibes. When exposed to a certain vibe long enough, the body (and mind) will fall into sync. If you've ever had a song bring you to tears or made you want to jump up and move, you get this.

A few years ago, several Binaural Beats products came on the market. Some websites were using popular drug culture language to promote sales. In contrast, others promised better sleep and the treatment of anxiety, stress, and related disorders. Of course, I had to try them.

What are Binaural Beats, and what's actually happening? I'm going to give you the very basics here because I'm not a physicist or sound expert. Basically, different tones are played into each ear, and the brain attempts to find a balance. Studies have yielded mixed results. Some say Binaural Beats are useful; some say they aren't. I used Binaural Beats regularly with an overall positive effect at the beginning of my mindfulness practice. I wasn't in the happiest place, and my mind wandered a lot to thoughts that made me anxious or depressed. This kind of sound focus work was a starting point for me. I think it would serve many who want to meditate but lack the resources or immediate ability to focus on learning how.

If you feel like you'd like to experiment with sound, look for what will motivate you in the direction you need to go. If you need to relax, what gets you there? That may be some classical, jazz, or old-school R&B. Is salsa, reggaeton, or hip hop what you play when you need to get up and go? Cool, but remember that you can expand your experience. Be open. Rain, bells, white noise, the ocean—there's a world of sound out there!

Have fun and use your ears to be well.

## Sight

Have you ever noticed how some people, many of them photographers, catch incredible moments? These are moments that most would miss, but these special people seem to see differently.

I was scrolling social media one day and stopped to admire a breathtaking photo. I was sure that this beautiful photo was taken in some exotic location, but the caption said no such thing. Instead it said, "North from my garage is a bush that catches the nicest raindrops and shows them off when the sun comes out, a broken watery bush of loveliness."

This was an image that I would have definitely missed. You see, at the time I was living in a place that I hated. I would later learn that the place I hated was truly more in my mind than anywhere else, but looking at that photo sparked something in me. Somewhere inside I knew that the ability to see the beauty in the most ordinary, even messy, places was a gift.

The dictionary says that sight is the process, power, or

function of seeing. Sight is a physical experience, but how the eye scientifically processes light has little to do with how we see things in the end. Some people have 20/20 vision, yet they don't really see what's going on. On the other hand, there are some blind people who see the world in ways that are inspiring, poetic, and prophetic. These people are intentional visionaries.

I've learned that vision is more than just a bunch of photons and electrical impulses in the eye. Images have to be processed through the big boss—the brain. Every day we're inundated with data. The brain ignores some data as "uninteresting" or "unimportant." Such ignored stimuli may have effects on the brain but don't reach consciousness.

As a result, we have a much easier time seeing things when we know what we're looking for. And we won't notice things that we're not familiar with or simply not searching for. "Perceptual blindness" is a term used by cognitive psychologists, and many of us are blind in some way or another.

What do you have around your home or even in your mirror that you're not seeing? Have you been blind?

Maybe.

The "invisible gorilla test" conducted by Daniel Simons and Christopher Chabris is the most popular introduction to perceptual blindness. The name alone gives it away, but in the test people are asked to count the number of basketball passes a team makes. In the middle of the video, a gorilla strolls right through the frame. In the original study, half of the people counting the passes missed it. I know I did. You can look this up and see for yourself whether the concept is valid in your case. Now that you know you're looking for a gorilla, you'll probably see it. Still, you may not be able to count the passes accurately because everyone has limited attention resources.

Change blindness is another type of blindness. It can occur

when objects are in clear (conscious) sight, and it happens over time. It's the idea that we often miss significant changes to our visual world from one view to the next. We're often not able to see changes that would be evident to someone who knows those changes are going to happen. What's really interesting is that some people notice these changes and other people don't, and we really don't yet have a good idea of what separates those who don't from those who do.

The brain's attention system allows us actively to select what to look at. It makes us very good at concentrating on tasks, but it can also make us miss something that's happening right in front of our eyes. Trees change color one leaf at a time, children grow to adulthood one day at a time. It would drive us practically crazy to notice every single change occurring in our world. Still, it isn't unusual to consider the possibility that we've been blind to great beauty, insight, or even miracles. Maybe, now that we're looking, we have a chance to see.

What do you want to see next?

You're an amazing being and have come equipped with a remarkable camera. It takes effort to look deeply into the visual clutter. However, once you turn your attention to what's before you, you discover all that you missed before.

The exercises here are meant to give you practice in looking deeply at what you might have ignored otherwise. As I've mentioned previously, I write almost everything down. If you feel so inclined, by all means, journal your observations. But it's fine to have each of these observations just as a stand-alone experience.

Wherever you are in the world, whatever the season, spot a flower. Grab a picture of yourself that you like. Why do you like it? What about this version of YOU do you enjoy? Is it the color you're wearing, the lighting, the way your head is tilted? How many shades of your favorite color can you spot in one day? When was the last time you watched a sunrise or sunset? Get thee to a sunset! Pick someone (a colleague, roommate, or child, etc.) you see every day. Decide to notice something different about them every day. Spot three different people laughing. How were they different from each other? How were they similar to you?

The Zen of sight observing or visual mindfulness is an enjoyable way of approaching the world. It may require a new way of thinking. Approaching each day with intention and purposefulness is the cornerstone of mindfulness. With mindfulness, we have a chance to learn to see the world as it is: as we make it. As we abandon dwelling in our past or future, we learn to live each moment in an authentic way.

## Smell

Now, I have a confession to make.

After my brain, my nose is the boss of me. I'm serious! My nose will often dictate what I eat, where I sit, and who I vibe with. There have been times when I felt the smell of something was so foul, I couldn't concentrate. At the point of gagging, I'd frantically ask if anyone knew the possible source, only to be told no one else smelled it! What? There was a hot funk literally taking over the space, and NO ONE else smelled it? I can't even! Moments later I would find that the garbage can across the street had been tipped over or a truck of fertilizer had driven by. My nose does not lie.

Mind you, not all smells are bad, right? I've also been driven near mad by a deliciously distracting smell. My nose has actually been thrust into a state of infatuation. Take, for instance, my crush on a makeup artist years ago. I was in the makeup chair on the set of a film I was working on. My makeup artist was a chubby, happy fellow who had a perm and wore lip gloss.

He was fabulous, but suffice to say, there wasn't any sexual interest on either side. However, when this man leaned over me and I got a whiff of the cologne he was wearing, it made me crazy. I asked him what it was and with haste bought some for my husband. The result? My husband smelled nice. Just nice.

Nice was NOT what I had in mind. NICE was NOT why I bought the cologne! I thought that when applied by my Zeus-like husband, this cologne would throw me into a frenzy. I was slightly disappointed. I realized that the scent of cologne isn't just about what's in the bottle. It's about the chemical reaction each individual has with it. I tried several colognes for Rico and myself. Still, with both of us sensitive to smell, I ultimately left it alone.

Fast forward almost twenty years. I was in the throes of a midlife crisis/revelation. Panic attacks. Bouts of depression. Many of you know the deal. At some point, I began to notice that the lotions, cleansers, and scents in my household were not me. Everything smelled more like a middle ground for what was acceptable to all five people living under my roof. I was annoyed. It was just another glaring area of compromise in my life.

More and more, I began to take an interest in aromatherapy for healing and pleasure. I then made a decision to again start trying little samples of colognes, perfumes, and oils. I discovered that most adverse reactions to cosmetics and toiletries are caused by fragrance chemicals, which are known irritants and allergens. If you've ever experienced sneezing, headaches, dizziness, coughing, rashes, and other skin irritations, it may just have been the synthetic fragrances in your products.

Today I regularly go on olfactory adventures. Sticking to natural fragrances eliminates any adverse reactions and allows me the freedom to explore. I mix and match. Some are good, some are bad, and BAM! I've found my IT group of smells.

One friend says my "it" smells like laundry. I don't get it, and I don't care because for the first time ever I'm mad about the smell of me!

Do you have a YOU fragrance? I'm not just talking about something that smells good, I'm talking about an aroma that can CHANGE your vibe; a scent that reminds you of how amazing and unique you are.

I urge you to start looking for it.

## Taste

Confucius said, "Everyone eats and drinks, yet only a few appreciate the taste of food."

Mindful eating is an everyday challenge for me. This is why I created a whole other chapter on eating in this book. In this chapter I focus just on the science.

Taste is basically a bundle of different sensations. Generally, the foods that we say taste good are ones we've been conditioned to like by our exposure to them. But did you know that the human sensory systems allow us to distinguish about 100,000 different flavors?

You read that right.

Taste can also be closely linked to our emotions. It's connected to the involuntary nervous system, which is why a bad taste can bring about vomiting or nausea. And flavors that are yummy not only make our mouth water, they can summon up nostalgia.

There's an old movie (well, it's old now but it was all the rage when I was coming up) called *9½ Weeks*. There's a scene where Mickey Rourke is feeding Kim Bassinger while she's blindfolded. The scene is incredibly erotic. There's a surrender of trust and a willingness to experience something new, even in the ordinary.

Your mouth has been made for so much more than just words. There are literally thousands of experiences waiting on the tip of your tongue. Exploring and expanding your ideas of what tastes good can be extremely sensual and rewarding. With or without someone else around.

I know I said I would try to stay scientific. I failed.

## Touch

For some of us, touch can be a blessing or a curse. It has become more apparent to me as I've worked with clients that our past life experiences play a huge part in our sensory experiences. Inappropriate touching and other forms of emotional or physical trauma can really fuck us up. It may take some time for some of us to learn how to give and receive the gift of touch, but the journey is worth it.

I grew up in a very touchy family. There were hugs and kisses but there were also slaps and ass whippings. The phrase "Mama don't take no mess" was definitely applicable to Carmen. She didn't shy away from putting her hands on people. A total stranger found this to be true in Boston. Mom was late to pick me up and I later found out that someone had snatched her bag and tried to run. Mom was chunky but she had started training for a marathon and, while she ran slow, she could run long. She chased this man for blocks, and when he got winded, she caught him and proceeded to beat the shit out of him. I'm pretty sure the police were called.

Carmen "La Loca" made it clear to everyone that she was not to be fucked with, but that woman was as affectionate as she was fierce. She was particularly great at hugging. As a kid,

I truly believed that her hugs were a cure for all kinds of heart-ache. Years later, I found out I wasn't wrong.

It turns out hugs are good for the heart. One study, conducted by Karen Grewen and Kathleen Light at the University of North Carolina, suggested that a daily dose of hugging protects adults from heart disease. Hugs increase the levels of oxytocin in both men and women. Oxytocin is the "love hormone," known to promote feelings of calm and closeness.

Researchers also discovered that women had reduced levels of cortisol following an embrace. Cortisol is a hormone produced by the adrenal glands as part of the body's response to stress. The fact that the female participants' cortisol levels were significantly lower means that women are exceptionally responsive to the calming effects of a hug. A hug a day can go a long way toward keeping a woman you love heart-healthy.

There was a movement in the early 2000s called the Free Hugs Campaign. It was started by Juan Mann and grew to people all over the world holding up signs that offered total strangers a free hug. The hugs were meant to be random acts of kindness—selfless acts performed just to make others feel better.

And it worked! International Free Hugs Day is celebrated on the first Saturday of July, but feel free to start a movement in your home. Start anywhere you think a hug can bring healing. For some, hugging may take some getting used to. I believe all hugs are powerful, even the long ones that at first may seem awkward. If you really give yourself in a hug, the simple gesture can have a profound impact on someone's emotional and physical health.

One of the many things Carmen "La Loca" also had an avid interest in was the healing power of massage. She was a certified masseuse and actually taught a class at the YWCA in the seventies. Mom was an intuitive woman, and she knew that there was something important about our ability to touch and be touched. She would bring me in as her demonstration model. She would explain the different techniques and show her students how to apply them.

There are conflicting opinions about the benefits of massage on the body, but I love a good massage. Research shows that massage therapy can help in varying populations with:

Anxiety

Depression

Poor quality of sleep

I want to write about the kinds of love that can be celebrated every day, with or without a partner. We're physical beings, and touch can be such a unique way to express love and promote physical wellness. So, treat yourself to some respect. Short on cash but got a skill or product? Try exchanging it for a massage! Give a massage, get a massage ... touch and be touched! Spread the love.

My last touch tip is something I came across in 2009. I was exploring various healing modalities and alternative ways to overcome states of anxiety, stress, insomnia, and depression. I came across Emotional Freedom Technique (EFT), or tapping. EFT combines the Eastern wisdom around acupressure, or meridian points, in our bodies, with traditional Western psychotherapy.

Sound freaky? It may be, but some swear by it and it's SO EASY. Like any other stress-reduction method, EFT isn't perfect and doesn't have a 100 percent success rate, but it has worked wonders for many.

Even bestselling author Jack Canfield, co-creator of the Chicken Soup for the Soul series, has teamed up with an EFT practitioner to produce a tapping event aimed to help people make emotional and physical breakthroughs. Nick Ortner, who organizes the annual Tapping World Summit, posted "Breakthroughs in Energy Psychology: A New Way to Heal the Body and Mind" on the Huffington Post. It's an interesting read, especially this bit: "In partnership with Dr. David Feinstein, Dr. Church (a Ph.D. who has been researching and using EFT since 2002) has been able to confirm that tapping on specific meridian points has a positive effect on cortisol levels."

There are tons of videos on YouTube, websites to check out, and practitioners you can find on Facebook. So the next time you feel stressed or overwhelmed by anything, consider TAPPING it away.

# Move It!

## Begin a love affair with your body.

WHEN SOMETHING WAS in her way, my mom used to say, "Move it or lose it!" The thing blocking her path could be an object or a person, and she could be quite bold, almost rude, in her demands.

Mom was only five feet tall, but she was thick and, as you might imagine, tough as nails. She was overweight for most of her adult life, and though it may sound crazy, it was something that I loved about her. As a kid, I would sink into my mom's body and feel so safe.

Ironically, being overweight myself terrified me. I was a chubby kid. When I was reunited with my mom in Boston after years of living with my dad, she took me to a pediatrician. I got on the scale and he very politely confirmed that I was overweight by five pounds. My mom never put me on a diet; instead, she asked if I would like to take dance or musical theater classes. As you know, I chose to dance. I lost the extra weight, but I'm sorry to say that I've spent most of my life afraid that I would always be the fat girl.

Here's a little piece of trivia. During the character development process for *Mi Vida Loca*, Seidy López, who played Mousie, and I discussed using real insecurities to create tension.

During the fire escape scene, Mousie screams "Ernesto will never love you with those fat-ass hips!" All 121 pounds of Sad Girl was furious, and that anger was fueled by the real-life anxieties of her maker.

To fully reap the joy of living in this physical world, I had to learn to make peace with my body. And with this truce, I had to learn to love this body and get to know it.

At fifty, I find myself less focused on form and more focused on function. That's not to say that I'm 100 percent free from the inner critic. Baby Gangsta can be cruel and holds steadfast to the idea of a perfect body. Her view is skewed by years of white, male-dominated advertising. She's unrealistic and never pleased. I'm never going to be Barbie, but somewhere in there this critic holds on to the idea that Barbie is what I should be. My best bet for dealing with her is to acknowledge her opinion. Then I remind her that I'm not focusing entirely on aesthetics today, but on my health.

Baby Gangsta is merely trying to help me. She wants to make sure that I can always catch a man. Because after all, as long as I can do that, I'll be okay. Even as I type this, I'm thinking to myself, "that shit sounds crazy. Why would I say something like that? This is supposed to be a book about empowerment!"

From the jump, I told you I was going to challenge beliefs. To do that, I have to share the truth about my own subconscious beliefs. The truth is that I'm most empowered when I can look deep into my views to find where some of my most damaging ideas are.

I don't move my body to look like Barbie. I move my body because I love my life. According to a report by the American Heart Association, the average American sits for six to eight hours per day. The average American is me! Like so many busy people, I can often lose track of time and end up working on my laptop and sitting all day. Sitting all day may not sound like a crime against the body, but think again. Sitting for long periods is connected to several health issues. Some of the problems related to sitting were even compared to smoking as a health risk! They include increased blood pressure, high blood sugar, and excess body fat around the waist, which is about more than looks. That extra fat also increases the risk of cardiovascular disease. Yes, people, studies have linked long periods of sitting with abnormal cholesterol levels and an increased risk for diabetes and even cancer.

As if the physical risks of sitting weren't enough, wouldn't you know that sedentary days have also been shown to increase anxiety! My previous chapter was ALL about anxiety and how I had to get over that shit. I needed to regain a healthy life for myself. This is why, even on days when I don't want to, I make it a point to get off my ass and move my body. I appreciate all that it allows me to do and experience, and I admit that the everyday appreciation for this body is sometimes an effort.

## "MOVEMENT IS A MEDICINE FOR CREATING CHANGE IN A PERSON'S PHYSICAL, EMOTIONAL, AND MENTAL STATES."

### – CAROL WELCH

Some of this journey is about feeling fabulous, and some of it is just about doing the work when you don't want to. When you decide that you're going to love yourself, your body, mind, and spirit are all a part of that equation, and there are actions that you'll have to take.

As I mentioned earlier, my journey into happiness started with me taking action to be well in body, mind, and spirit. Many of the Eastern practices unite the physical and spiritual movement. Take yoga, for example. I've heard yoga described as prayer in motion. The indigenous people of Africa and the Americas have used dance communication with spirit since the beginning of time. In Hawaii, hula links the Hawaiians with the Universe and makes them one with all creation. The Bible says King David danced before the Lord with all his might—in his underwear, no less!

I can't possibly tell you what kind of movement your soul craves, but I truly believe that somewhere inside each of us is the body's desire to move.

My workouts vary. Some days exercise is a chore, but most days I really like it. I try to schedule walks with my boo or my kids at the end of the day. When I've done what I needed to do to get my blood flowing and be connected with my loved ones, I feel good about it.

I don't like the gym, but I do like a set of resistance bands my homegirl gifted me. I love to dance and ride my bike, and when it's warm I really like to hit the pool. I love to hike, but I don't get out to do it regularly. I could do it more often, but the truth is that I don't, so I don't beat myself up about it. I use a step tracker so that I consciously remember to move my body every single day.

I also try to stretch every morning. Until I was in my forties I didn't realize how important flexibility is to overall health. Increasing flexibility is one of the fundamentals of fitness. If you aren't physically fit or used to stretching, I HIGHLY recommend you take a class or try some of the great resources available online and in person. I thank my mother every day for putting me in dance class, and I thank my stars that I loved it. I see a chiropractor as often as possible. I like to have my joints and bones stretched and put back in order! I'm still pretty flexible.

Walking is my go-to move. In 2001, after the birth of my

second child, I had the baby blues. I had gained sixty pounds even though she weighed less than six. Do the math. I had never been overweight in my life, and what was worse, I was depressed and unmotivated. Rico's incessant questions about my workout didn't help motivate me. In fact, because I was such an emotional wreck, it just made me more insecure. He was a fitness trainer with gobs of knowledge about how the body works. He knew that getting the blood circulating through the body was an essential factor in overcoming even emotional conditions. However, because I was depressed, I just grew more and more convinced he found me disgusting.

It didn't help that a woman I considered a mentor would pull me aside and repeatedly tell me that my husband would be more "encouraged" if I got in shape. WTF? I was nursing and still running my household. I was raising a seven-year-old kid and working full-time after only twelve weeks at home with my newborn baby. And by the way, I was also hella guilty about feeling depressed when I had a beautiful, healthy baby girl. Sometimes well-meaning people have no idea that they're adding insult to injury with their "helpful" comments.

And do you know what's worse? We're frequently the ones who trained them to speak to us in a certain way! We often surround ourselves with people who support our subconscious beliefs. Can you see how this woman ignited my fear of being the fat girl? Her comments endorsed Baby Gangsta's point that I needed to look a specific way to be attractive to a man. She was just nudging me back into the role that I had created for myself. Unfortunately, that role didn't include a place for me to learn how to love and accept myself unconditionally.

I never found the words to share with her how her suggestions affected me. The script for me in 2001 would have read, "Lady, I'm struggling with wanting to brush my teeth, so thinking of someone else's needs right now doesn't provide any motivation AT ALL. As a matter of fact, it makes things worse. So if you wanna help, instead of urging me to get in shape, go tell THAT muthafucker to step the fuck up and help me! Do THAT, and maybe I'll feel just a tad less shitty than I do! How 'bout that?"

That would have been delivered with a lot of hand gesturing followed up with an eye roll.

The main problem with this script is that it's still outer-focused. Expecting that Rico's actions could fix me was a recipe for disaster. It again put a solution to what ailed me in the hands of someone else. I won't invalidate the script from 2001 because at least I would have gotten some essential points across. I was overwhelmed, depressed, and angry.

But 2001 Angel didn't speak at all. Frankly, she was afraid to even hint about some of the things she was thinking. Such dark thoughts can spring from a mind affected by hormones and stress. So those scripts were kept in the vault. I should have seen a doctor, but postpartum 2001 Angel stuffed her pain and confusion. She didn't complain, she just took on the new role that she assigned herself and kept pushing.

This wrecked me emotionally and physically. I was exhausted. I won't invalidate that experience because, while it didn't teach me how to stand up for myself, it did show me that I can make it through hard times. I now know what it takes to make it through some of the chemical havoc that can occur after birth.

The current version of Angel is more me-centric. That may seem selfish to some, but this version of myself helps more people. It's ironic but true. Today I aim to keep the right balance of boldly creating and expressing my boundaries while still being open to learning. To be honest, I can't say for sure what my script today would be. Part of my growth process is not expecting perfection from myself or anyone else. Still, I'm hoping that I've done enough work that if I ran across someone who gave me the same advice now, my words would support my purpose:

*I believe that you're trying to help me, but right now I feel like reducing the amount of pressure in my life. Currently, I'm focusing on myself and only surrounding myself with people who don't ask me to give more than I have to give. I really need to figure out how to love and accept this new body and mind. I've always respected and admired you. I hope you can empathize with where I'm at. If not, I hope we can meet up in the future when I'm hormonally balanced and adjusted to the newest version of myself.*

That's what I would like to say. Something level-headed and sophisticated. But I'd be lying if I said I could guarantee anything beyond, "Are you fucking kidding me?" After all, I'm still a work in progress!

I shared this story with you for a few reasons. Number one is that I learned so much about myself from that time. Through all of my growing pains, I've learned to be more compassionate toward others as well as myself. I try to remember that we all come to every relationship with baggage and that we all have a Baby Gangsta. I can't be sure how everyone's subconscious mind talks to them or what it has to say, but I know we all have chatter.

They say hindsight is 20/20. Looking back, I realize that this woman—while a brilliant professional, wife, mother, and minister—was just advising me based on her own limited frame of reference. Maybe she was dealing with body-love issues herself. Perhaps she didn't recognize signs of postpartum depression. I know that her desire to protect my marriage was genuine, and today I understand that she wanted to help. I'm pretty sure that I've said some things from my own frame of reference that either hurt people or turned them off. Thank goodness for grace and forgiveness. It allows us to move past pain and reminds us to be humble. We're all on a journey of learning and growth.

The second point of this story is to let you know that I ultimately did begin to feel better. Slowly but surely, I learned to surrender to a healthier mindset. I gained this gift by understanding that my mental wellness and physical fitness were more connected to each other than I realized. The journey to this realization started when my daughter was about ten months old. On a rare day, a combination of my mom's gentle coaxing and the Los Angeles sun led me to take a stroll. At a local drug store, I found a series of videos called "Walk Away the Pounds" by Leslie Sansone. They were on super sale, and for some reason I bought them. Those videos were perfect. I had stayed in good shape up until my second child, but suddenly I found myself too tired and too embarrassed to go to the gym or a class. Those videos were comfortable enough that, although I was panting, I victoriously completed the entire first video on my first try. My first walk lasted maybe ten minutes, but the feeling of victory was what I needed to get on the road to recovering my physical health. Winning is an important experience in a health plan, but by far the most essential experience is love.

Over the past nearly twenty years I've learned that to sustain a healthy body long term, I need to learn to love it and accept it as it is and as it changes. This is an everyday commitment. Why? Why do I, a fifty-year-old woman, need a daily practice of conscious body love and acceptance to be happy? Maybe because humans love beauty but standardize it in really bizarre ways. We have media trends and filters and surgery and all kinds of things luring us to be different from what we are.

There's no formula for what it looks like to truly love yourself. There are large women with no health problems who hate their bodies, there are small women with no health problems who hate their bodies. Some old women love their bodies, and some young women love their bodies. Some have had surgery and hate their bodies. Some have NOT had surgery and hate their bodies.

You get the point. Love may be inspired or enhanced by the outside, but it must live on the inside. However big, small, old, young, perfect, or imperfect someone seems, no one can fake love for the long term.

There's a connection between my body and my creator, and it's love. This, perhaps, had the most significant impact on my desire to joyfully move. For years I had relied on vanity for motivation. Now love and gratitude have replaced my desire to look a particular way to prove that I'm worthy. This is something that I continue to revisit as I get older and continue living a public life.

I began moving regularly again because I chose to love my body. I wasn't inspired because it was fat or ugly or because it would make my then husband feel aroused. I decided to thank my body for all that it had been through over the years.

I attended a talk where a young lady announced that she stood naked in front of the mirror and loved herself. It took me almost fifteen years after I started loving my body to take that step. Today I ask my body for forgiveness when I'm comparing myself to someone else and become critical of myself. My body has served me and I'm grateful.

When I first started to move my body again, a good friend noticed that I was feeling better. Although I'd lost weight, she didn't say, "Oh, Angel, you lost weight, you look great!" She said, "Oh, Angel! It's so good that you were able to get your qi moving! Your energy is beautiful!"

I wondered what the heck she was talking about. So I

looked it up. For the Chinese, qi (pronounced, "chee," is the life-force or energy in the world. The fundamental insight of Chinese medicine is that balanced and free-flowing qi results in health.

In contrast, stagnant or imbalanced qi leads to disease. We tend to think of disease as critical medical conditions, but break the word down and you see that (dis)ease is a state of being uncomfortable. My friend recognized that I was comfortable in my body. I was healthy, and it was beautiful for her to see me feeling good about myself.

In May 2009, a Harvard Medical School health publication said, "Tai chi ... might well be called 'medication in motion.' There is growing evidence that this mind-body practice ... has value in treating or preventing many health problems."

Oh yes, my qi moved, and for me walking was not only energizing—it was therapeutic.

When I got pregnant with my son, I was scared that I might have postpartum depression again. I wrote notes to myself. I sealed the letters so I could read them to myself after I gave birth. The notes reminded me that the chemical imbalances would eventually subside. They said that no matter how sad I felt, I could always walk. Mostly, I just wanted to let myself know that I could get through whatever came my way. As life would have it, having my son was a smooth experience. No postpartum at all. I was up and moving as soon as he was born.

There have been points in my life when I wanted to just do nothing—you know, sit on my couch and veg out. That's okay every once in a while. But there's not a doubt in my mind that stagnant qi will lead to disease.

If you come to any of the workshops I do, there's always a section for moving qi. I place the qi-mover smack dab in the middle of the workshop. I use a lot of physical humor in my delivery so that people will loosen up and not be intimidated to try something new. I've brought in some excellent instructors and introduced yoga, dance, and Paida to some pretty diverse audiences. No matter what we do, the qi-mover never fails to shift the energy in the room.

It's easy to underestimate the power of moving the body. Sometimes the busier we get, the further down on the priority list we put our physical fitness. It helps me to remember that working out is not for vanity, it's for sanity. Like for so many of my busy comadres, one of my challenges has been scheduling time. I read a quote that said, "You will never find time for anything. If you want time, you must make it." This is a hard one, especially for a woman who has had all sorts of expectations placed on her. Trust me, I know. The list of shit that a Latina, mom, daughter, wife, community leader, employee, business owner has to take care of …

You see the menu that comes up under all the titles we carry and hats we wear? It's long.

Somewhere in there we have to decide that we'll make time for the meat suit that's hosting our party. A swim, a dance, a hike, a class—SOMETHING. If you work at a desk, schedule yourself several times to move. If you need to put on some headphones and dance or walk or stretch, make time for it.

Also, try to have some fun! Just because you're a grown-up doesn't mean you have to be serious all the time. Have you ever noticed how children naturally enjoy jumping on a bed?

My kids were total jumping beans. During one of our moves, I dismantled their beds so we could get them to the new house. One day I noticed that the kids were having the best time jumping on their mattresses. Out of habit, I was about to stop them, and then I thought, *Why?* With their mattresses on the floor, they were safer than on a bed several feet up, and I was having such a good time watching them giggle, I decided to join them.

Just like the astronauts' experience while floating in space, I felt my body in a state of weightlessness at the top of the bounce. I hadn't felt so free in a while. The workout was quite good too, so I decided to do some investigating. I found out that jumping is excellent for the body. Jumping on a mini-trampoline can be an effective workout for children and also grown-ass women who want to have a little fun!

The body wants to be loved and moved. Love it, and it will continue to serve you in such beautiful ways. Depending on your current physical condition, there will be different options for you. I want to give a special shout-out to my people out there in wheelchairs or other limited physical conditions. You are whole! Whatever level of mobility you have, celebrate it. If you can move your hands or blink your eyes, do so with consciousness, gratitude, and love.

I met a young lady a few years ago who had suffered a stroke and required years of physical therapy. She started by moving her pinky. Today, while she can walk, she still has some limitations, but she motivates and inspires others like you wouldn't believe.

Motivational speaker Nick Vujicic is another person who comes to mind when I think of people who may appear to be limited. He was born without any limbs. As a kid he contemplated suicide, but something in him said, "NO! I will not give up." He is now joyful and inspires millions of people. He reminds me that each and every one of us is full of infinite potential. You're here for a reason. Your limitations don't define you, and they shouldn't keep you from loving your body.

And let's not forget our faces. Yes, friends, that face of yours needs attention, too. Once again, I have to thank my mom, the brilliant Carmen Reyes Aviles, for showing me the way to stay young-looking! Facial muscles are involuntary, and they reflect whatever we're feeling. So be conscious about where you hold tension in your face.

I've been told that I looked mean when I thought I was just neutral. I didn't grow up in a smiley sort of place, so it has taken me a long time to have a relaxed facial expression that doesn't look mad. The cool thing is that we can work on counter muscles to tone up the one area that can't be hidden behind clothes!

Yoga, aerobics, weight training, and stretching aren't for your bodies alone. By contracting and relaxing muscles on your neck and face, you can boost circulation, improve muscle tone, and release excess tension.

Try the following exercises to soften wrinkles, lines, and creases that already exist and prevent new ones from forming. You may feel ridiculous at first, BUT the results may keep you from appearing older than your age.

### Fishy/Kissy Face

Purse your lips. Open and close like a fish eating food.

### Eyes-Wide-Open Aerobics

Look around in circles. Look as far in all directions around the rim of the eye. Repeat five to ten times.

### Neck Aerobics

Also known as the underbite! Have you ever seen how a bulldog's underbite looks? That's our goal, too. Look up at a 45-degree angle. Take the bottom row of your teeth and stretch them up over your top lip. Repeat fifteen to twenty times.

## Smile-High Club

This is the most subtle and controlled exercise. Maybe you haven't noticed, but a lot of us smile from the lower part of our facial cheeks. Try smiling with just the apples of your cheeks. Your upper lip will lift and stretch. You'll probably feel like the Joker.

## Yoga Lion Variation

The lion is a yoga position that uses the entire body. Carmen would do just the face part. Open your mouth wide and let out an audible sigh. Stretch your tongue out as far as possible. Repeat this three times, then relax.

Finally, my mom encouraged me to just be expressive. Laughing, smiling, gasping all utilize the face muscles. So let your next workout be about FACE!

It's my firm belief that we were meant to move our bodies and that we were meant to love it. Throughout history we've been sold a great campaign of shame. In this chapter, I'd like to claim one day a year when we throw into a virtual toilet all the shit we've come to believe about how imperfect we are and give it a good FLUSH.

Let's call it "Sin Vergüenza Day!" *Sin vergüenza* means *shameless*. Let's start being shameless about our bodies' shapes and sizes, and the condition of our skin, hair, and nails.

In some cases, let's just admit that we've not always made the best choices for these incredible machines. Let's commit today to do the best we can. Sin Vergüenza Day is the best day of the year because it's a day we get to devote to fully loving ourselves. On Sin Vergüenza Day, there are no mirrors and there are no visual media. Just full-on time alone with ourselves. We love and accept our bodies because it's good for us.

That's it. Keep it moving.

# Eat, Drink, And Be Merry

## Paying attention to consumption improves quality of life.

*N*ow it's time to dive into one of my favorite subjects in life: FOOD!

I'm all about living life to the fullest. I enjoy foods that are part of my culture and those that have become traditions in my home. With that being said, this chapter is about food, but it's not written by a nutritionist. I'm just a fifty-year-old woman who's in good health and loves to share what she's learning. I admit that a lot of what I've learned has been sourced from books I've read or articles I've found online. But even more important for me is figuring out what works with my body. You can choose paleo, keto, vegan, kosher, Atkins, Scarsdale… the list of trendy diets is endless. In this chapter, I hope to inspire you to listen to your body and use wisdom in its care.

I've always wanted to stay in shape, first as an actress, then as the wife of an athlete. However, I became passionate about nutrition because of my beautiful son. He had a dietary restriction that made me want to know all I could about using food as medicine. It's incredible to me that many of us walk around and don't even know that we may be allergic to the foods we eat.

And it's not just about allergies. There are all sorts of intolerances to so many foods. I've known some people who experienced years of discomfort before discovering their ailment was nutrition-related. Some of you reading this right now struggle with never feeling 100 percent physically well. Food intake may be a whole study in and of itself for you.

Throughout my life I've eaten almost everything offered to me. I've eaten raw meats, animal brains, chocolate-covered bugs, and loads of other things—sometimes on a dare, sometimes just because. I have, indeed, done it all.

## "LET FOOD BE THY MEDICINE AND MEDICINE BE THY FOOD."

### – HIPPOCRATES

When I was pregnant with my first child, I went from being a plant-leaning omnivore to a beefatarian. Make no mistake, I paid the price about a year later. I was in a small desert town in California, shooting an independent film. I was having a blast on this gig as the only female among the talented Alfred Molina, Ruben Blades, Esai Morales, and Matthew McConaughey. Then, out of the blue I suddenly felt constipated and bloated.

The town's population was about one thousand, with around 85 percent being retired. There were no places to hang out, but there was a large pharmacy. I was twenty-six and invincible, so I sucked up the discomfort and filled up on GasX, Tums, and anything else I could find.

Two days later I had a fever and couldn't sit up straight. The producer first took me to see a local doctor who assumed the film we were working on was porn. He prescribed penicillin for the bogus venereal disease diagnosis. He told us to go to the hospital if my symptoms didn't subside.

The hospital was over an hour away. I know because I ended up there with a ruptured appendix. The doctor who performed my surgery explained that my body had experienced trauma and that, in his opinion, I should consider a vegetarian diet. It was a wake-up call for twenty-six-year-old me. The irony? Mom had tried to raise a vegetarian from the beginning!

I told you, my family was not your average Puerto Rican, from-the-hood family. We had the usual loud, loving, food-filled family gatherings seen in movies that stereotype our culture. We had all the crazy characters that made it fun, like the aunt who was always mad at or cussing out somebody, and a grandmother who would ask you to say "when" and insist on serving two additional spoonfuls on your plate. There were the obligatory dramatic episodes instigated by teen pregnancies, addictions, and jail time. This was life in the South Bronx in the seventies. It could be wild and unpredictable, but it was typical for that place and time.

Overall, my extended family was pretty average, so most of the eccentricity came from Mom and her offspring. She was an oddball. She was raised in the hood and would beat your ass in a minute, but she was also book smart. From the earliest I can remember, Carmen was always reading about something, but one of her favorite subjects was food.

She had over a hundred cookbooks and had collected thousands of recipes from magazines. At some point, Mom discovered that vegetarianism was better for the body. This, however, wasn't a notion she could make stick in our household. My dad loved pork, and he was willing to die for a chop. I also had an Italian babysitter who thought Mom was nuts. Mom would often find me at Italia's house with a chicken leg in one hand

and a glass of wine and water in the other. Still, Mom tried to bring in Italia's kitchen wizardry.

In our kitchen Mom was somewhat of a mad scientist. She was an incredible baker and could make magic from seemingly impossible combinations of ingredients. She was always experimenting with things. She would make her own yogurt and fermented drinks. One year she got something called a biosnacky, and we had every kind of sprout you could think of.

Mom would often go into phases of styles and devote a year or more to a particular culture. These journeys into other cultures by way of food led to more studies and were by far one of the best gifts my mom gave me. Every year or so, she would take an area and focus on sharing the food, music, art, and history. She would always say that one day when I had the money and time to travel, I would be able to appreciate the places I visited. Mom hoped that this exposure would make me an open-minded person with respect for all cultures. She also reminded me that learning requires resources, and if you don't have the money, you must use your brain. She would often grab books from the library and scan local papers for free cultural events.

One year mom chose India. On weekends we would maybe go to the East Village in New York City and have a traditional Indian lunch. We might buy spices at an Indian market in Jersey or have a neighbor help us buy fabric and learn to tie a sari. We might watch a Bollywood film, or take a yoga class, or listen to Ravi Shankar and make curry at home. Mom really liked to mix it up so that I could have a sense that the world is a big place, full of people who do things differently but are also very much the same.

I didn't physically travel much with Mom, but she opened my eyes and palate to the world. On our world tours through her kitchen, I learned to love Indian as well as Japanese, North

African, Caribbean, Chinese, and American soul food and culture. Although my mom had traveled through Mexico, she didn't expose me to Mexican cuisine. But trust and believe that I made up for that when I moved to Los Angeles. Let me tell you, my love for food from all parts of Mexico is borderline obsessive. My kids have actually been raised eating Mexican food more than anything else.

In the last few years, I've mostly stuck to a diet that's about 90 percent plant-based. What does that mean? For me, it means more than just not eating meat. It means that I eat amazing meals that I think about, try to plan for, and prepare at home. I don't usually eat meat, but I will have an occasional piece of fish that my love Rey caught in Alaska. I will also eat out and not flip out if a cookie I eat is made with butter, or the broth in a meal is made from meat. I'm trying to live a more conscious way of life for myself and the rest of the planet. I'm not here to judge others; I'm here to share what I've learned on the road to my happy place and to encourage you to find yours.

Essential to feeling on top of my game is incorporating a LIVING-food meal daily. What are living foods? They're foods that still contain enzymes because they haven't been heated over 116 degrees. Living and raw foods usually have higher nutrient values than foods that have been cooked. Most people imagine a salad when they think raw. Yes, salad is an option, but there are so many more. There are many cookbooks and online recipes out there to help you pair flavors and nutrients for simple and delicious meals.

I do at least one living-food shake a day for myself and my household. Please note that I live with my kids and significant other, but I often have visitors come in from out of town, so they're also subject to my mad scientist shakes!

In addition to Mexican food, I will also confess my addiction to shakes. I make or purchase SOME form of shake every day. Some of the combinations have been delicious and some ... not so delicious. I've learned to test the combos out myself before I serve them up to kids and guests. My ex was a body-builder, so my kids have been drinking shakes since they were young. They're teens now, and in some ways they're pickier than ever, but they'll still gulp down a shake if I serve it in the morning.

Doctors urge us all to eat at least five fresh fruit and veggie servings per day—and there is no way my kids will do it if I don't put it in their face! One day, when my kids were about eight and ten, I made an acai (frozen and available in stores or online) smoothie. I wanted to double up on protecting their immune systems, so I added an antioxidant berry mix plus fresh blackberries, kale, and spirulina.

The result looked like petroleum oil. To kids, looks matter, and my kids didn't want any part of this. (For a shake that's a total kid-pleaser, check out Trinity's Purple Passion or the Think Green Shake on my blog.) Spirulina can have an almost fishy smell, so I used half a tablespoon for an entire blender. The sweetness from the antioxidant berry mix, which included cherries, helped cut the bitterness from the kale (I only used three leaves). It wasn't the most delicious of my shake recipes, but it was in no way as wrong as it looked! Still, it was a no-go for the kids. So the next time, I used blueberries instead of blackberries, and they drank it down and have been drinking living smoothies ever since.

Another key to making sure the smoothie is healthy is to monitor the sugar. I use coconut water instead of juice and make sure that I'm not providing too many sugary fruits in one serving. This used to be a burden, but now all things are labeled. You can also quickly look up something's sugar content on your phone.

**ONCE YOU CAN FEED ON THE LIVING ENERGY,
YOUR LUNGS WILL BE IN AN EXTRAORDINARY
STATE OF CLEAR, COOLNESS.
FORGET THE SPIRIT, AND THERE ARE
NO APPEARANCES TO CLING TO;
MERGE WITH THE ULTIMATE,
AND THE EXISTENT EMPTINESS IS GONE.
FOR BREAKFAST LOOK FOR WILD TARO ROOTS;
WHEN HUNGRY AT NIGHT, PICK WETLAND MUSHROOMS.
IF YOU MIX IN SMOKE AND FIRE,
YOUR BODY WILL NOT WALK ON THE JEWEL POND.**

**-TAOIST POEM**

Well, if that isn't the most explicit reason to eat raw food, I don't know what is! However, I did start off this book by saying that I'm NOT a guru. I may never actually walk on a jewel pond. In all honesty, I still don't really know what that means, but put simply, eating more raw food is beneficial to your body, mind, and spirit. You just need to try to do it as much as possible. You may never make it as a monk. Still, living foods will add to the quality of your life by boosting immunity, reducing healing time, facilitating the elimination of toxins, and, last but not least, giving you radiant skin.

I think it's crucial for me to briefly touch on the fact that our food isn't the same as what I grew up on. In the last seventy years, food has become more readily available but a lot less nutritious. These days, believe it or not, 85 percent of Americans lack essential vitamins. A study in 2004 published by the National Center for Biotechnology Information compared US Department of Agriculture data on vegetable nutrients from 1950 to data from 1999 and found notable decreases, particularly for critical nutrients like calcium, iron, phosphorus, riboflavin, and ascorbic acid.

The same goes for meat. For example, grass-fed and organic beef is nutritionally different from factory-farmed, processed meat. Sadly, this means that you have to either grow food yourself or live in an area where real, organic products are available.

Organics are notoriously expensive, but if you have access to certain ingredients, eating a low-processed, plant-based diet can be affordable. Rice and beans from scratch are a perfect example of a plant-based meal that's cheaper than meat. Still, the carbs are high, and to create balance you would need access to nutritious, live food.

Finding vital ingredients can be a challenge—especially if you live in a food desert. Food deserts exist in communities throughout the United States and are defined as places with little to no access to fresh fruit, vegetables, and other healthful whole foods.

The word *undernourished* may have you picturing skinny babies in other parts of the world. However, in the United States, the picture of undernutrition is different. In some cases, you can spot people who are both obese and malnourished. They're consuming foods that are calorie-dense but nutritionally deficient. It's called "hidden hunger," and it can lead to both physical and mental health issues.

Poverty is not just material. In my humble opinion, ignorance is the biggest culprit in our loss of power over our mental, physical, and spiritual health. When I think of a beautiful body, I don't have in mind someone skinny. I have in mind someone healthy, enjoying an active life, and, most of all, disease-free.

There's a body-positivity movement that promotes the love of the body in all shapes and sizes. I love this because, as someone who struggled with paralyzing self-criticism, I'm 100 percent for teaching us all how to love who we are. For me, true love is a balancing act. I can eat what I like and also eat what's right for my body. We have to have certain nutrients in our bodies and eat in a way that provides sustaining nutrition.

My final thoughts about food are to eat with consciousness. I don't think you have to pray over every meal to communicate with God or prove you're grateful, but there's a reverence for food that has gone missing. Fast food is so easy and requires so little thought that we can be almost unconscious eaters. If I eat meat or veggies, or just suck up air, the one thing I hope I can be is conscious. My greatest desire is to promote getting rich in mind, body, and spirit.

I recognize how privileged I am to live in a place that offers so many choices. And it's a double blessing that I can afford some of those choices. Living in Los Angeles is expensive. I've served the homeless, and I've had times when I've barely been able to scrape by myself. Humbling circumstances sometimes make us more empathetic people. I've come to learn that not everyone at a soup kitchen is there because they're on drugs. Eating is a privilege, even in a luxe city like Los Angeles. The least I can do is pay attention to what I ingest.

Now, didn't I say eat, DRINK and be merry? Let's get to the fun part: drinking!

My drink of choice? Get ready for it ... water! Civilizations have been built around it; gods have reigned over it, and poets have been inspired by it. Skeptics can argue the legitimacy of claims of specific belief systems or science. Still, little can be refuted when it comes to the importance of water to the human race. We need water to live on. Plain and simple.

I'm one of the lucky people who like water. I drink tons of it. I'll sometimes flavor it with cucumber or fruit. I'll drink it cold or hot with a slice of lemon. Mostly though, I just drink it as it is. I carry a bottle in my bag as well as in the car. When people ask me about my skin and how I keep it so young looking, I say, "It's a combination of mindset, genetics (thanks, Mom), and WATER!"

You might be thinking that genetics and water make sense, but mindset? Yep. I call it conscious consumption. Water is life. For me and everyone I know, access to water is fundamental. But for some people, access to water isn't easy. I learned this first-hand on several occasions.

One in particular stands out. Operation Hydration started out as a simple mission to do something useful during the summer of 2016. My friend Nina Womack had coordinated a festival and had a surplus of water just taking up space in storage. Nina is one of the most giving people I know, and while she could have sold those bottles, she wanted to do something positive for the community. We decided that we would hydrate the homeless.

The homeless population in Los Angeles was tens of thousands of people, so Nina and I met to discuss ways to deliver as much water to as many people as possible. We decided to make the event public. So many groups and individuals from all over the country were inspired to help, it was humbling. The project grew beyond our wildest expectations, and a full documentary was created as a public art project for the City of Los Angeles, Department of Cultural Affairs.

As a side note, I have to mention that volunteerism gives me life. There's something deeply spiritual about service. The lessons I've learned through service couldn't have been learned any other way. The gifts I've received while serving someone who can't pay me back include, but aren't limited to, humility, gratitude, and encouragement. It's been so much fun to witness how the Universe pays back service exponentially. The exchange of smiles is worth millions. The connection is like winning the lottery. It wasn't easy to broadcast that we wanted to do something good. Servants usually want to keep things on the down-low, but sometimes, to make the most significant impact, we need to open our mouths, share what we're doing, and ask for help.

We had done a lot of research for Let's Be Whole, which is Nina's organization. We learned some staggering statistics about the state of the planet. We also realized how important water is to every aspect of our health. Did you know that a human can survive without food for quite some time but can go only about three days without water? If we can get to that three-day limit, our brain strains to keep us conscious. Severe dehydration can cause life-threatening complications like heat-stroke and low blood-volume shock. If you're thirsty, you're already dehydrated—and even mild dehydration can lead to fatigue, muscle weakness, dizziness, mood shifts, muddled thinking, and memory loss. Another symptom of dehydration is headaches. There are lots of other causes of these problems, of course, but dehydration is a common one.

During Operation Hydration, we realized that a person who's on medication, using drugs, or drinking alcohol can quickly dehydrate and not even know it. Many of the home-less brothers and sisters we served recognized that dehydration exacerbated the mental health conditions on the streets. They also told us that access to water was getting harder and harder for some of them.

As of the time of my writing, California is the world's fifth-largest economy, and our homeless population is the highest in the nation. The state's human right to water law stipulates that every person has the right to safe, clean, affordable, and accessible water for drinking, cooking, and sanitation. But the unsheltered homeless are still dealing with dire water conditions.

California is not alone.

Did you know that almost a billion people don't have access to clean drinking water? As reported by UNICEF in 2013, almost two thousand children under the age of five die every day because they lack uncontaminated water. This isn't the current reality in many places, but we can't get it twisted; there's a war being waged over the Earth's drinking water. And the United States isn't immune. The people of Flint, Michigan, have experienced a water crisis first-hand. The Sioux tribe has been protesting the Dakota Access Pipeline because it threatens the water supply in four states. Many people say that the pipeline will create jobs and bring wealth to the area, but we should all evaluate what real wealth means. Google the value of water, and you'll find that water is actually a trillion-dollar industry.

My intention is not to turn this book into a liberal political rant. I honestly just want to focus on the well-being of as many people as possible. I believe that wellness is a concept that has broader applications than just us as individuals. In other words, as we get well, we allow for an expansion of consciousness. We don't overwhelm ourselves with problems that we can't fix. Still, we find ways to modify our own behaviors in ways that add to the collective wellness of all.

In closing this chapter, I want to urge you to consume more consciously. Do it because it's right for you and, as a bonus, it benefits the planet. Form a water habit if you can. Keep a reusable bottle in your car, in your purse, on your desk, and by your bed. Drink it! Set a reminder on your phone or via email, or have your kids or friends text you. I have a GIANT thermos that's always full of tea. I drink all kinds of tea. I put one bag in and just keep refilling with hot water.

Do your own thing, and from now on, when you drink that glass of water, I hope you can thank your god if you have one, your lucky stars, your city, your plumber, and yourself.

I hope you're connected to all the possibilities that abound, because in drinking that water, you've chosen to live.

LIFE is a miracle. I hope your subconscious mind decides to believe that.

# *Act Up!*

## How vision, emotion and movement can build momentum for change.

*N*OW IT'S TIME to get ready for your close-up. A few chapters back, you had the chance to become the scriptwriter of your own life. In this chapter you're going to learn some acting techniques that will help you take your script to the next level.

When I was learning these things back in the day, I had no idea that I would be using them to help people all over the world learn to live better, more satisfying lives. I am so grateful.

This chapter is all about visualization, imagination, and feeling. Alone, these are some compelling tools, but together they give you a total, make-some-shit-happen cocktail! What a fun technique this is, but believe it or not, some people have a tough time doing it. In my workshops I always save this part for last. From experience, I know that some people care more about looking foolish than they do about potentially opening up to something brilliant, healing, or fun.

We're often taught that we're wasting our time when we play, but that's just because we aren't aware of how important creativity can be. So many people use their imagination every day without even knowing it. And some people imagine the worst things. You probably know a few people who worry about everything that can go wrong; they seem to be or know the unluckiest people on the planet.

Most kids love to play and use their imagination, and they're amazing—most of them can jump into a world of play and stay there for hours. I was one of those kids. As early as I can remember, my imagination far superseded any toys or games I could be gifted. I would play elaborate dress-up games with my best friend, Annette. We did the most, let me tell you. She would come up to my house with a bag full of old clothes and costumes, and we would play for hours. From an apartment in the Bronx, we would launch ourselves into outer space or jet around the globe to attend fancy parties.

As "luck" would have it, years later Annette and I both went on to travel the world and attend some pretty fantastic events. Go figure!

I also found a wonderful playmate in Nana, my maternal grandmother. She would take me to the park, and we would play for hours. I would run Nana through a battery of questions about her travels around the world, and she would patiently indulge me.

Although I had never set foot in an airport, Nana would explain to me in detail what her travel experiences had been. My games always included all of the things Nana described. I would pretend to be in line to board the aircraft and make sure to say hello to the pilot.

One of my favorite games to play with Nana was "Going to the Bahamas." Nana's elaborate descriptions of turquoise waters and powdery, white sand were enough to keep me outside for hours. And while a winter coat covered my body in New York City, my mind was far away on a tropical island. When I was thirteen, Nana did take me to the Bahamas, and it was just like I pictured it, but better.

I don't know if Nana knew what a refuge she was for me— what her playful indulgence did for my mind, body, and spirit. She was not an educated woman. It's doubtful Nana had more than a second-grade education. She was Venezuelan, and her family had no money, so she chose to leave her home country at fourteen. Nana worked on a plantation in Trinidad for seven years, learned to speak English, and saved up enough money to arrive in New York City with twenty-three dollars in her pocket.

She worked hard. Her first few years away from home were focused on sending any extra money back home. She was determined to send her younger siblings to school. Once ensuring that her two younger brothers were secure, Nana sent for Wela, my great-grandmother.

Somewhere in there, Nana managed to marry a scoundrel and give birth to my mom. The only thing my grandfather provided was genetics. People say I look like him, but I don't see it. He took off on his family, and that's what I think of when I look at his picture. I used to judge him so harshly— especially after my sister and I found letters from him asking my grandmother to send him money. Can you imagine? My grandmother was a four-foot-eleven, dark-skinned woman who worked in a factory! He was a fair-skinned man. His earning potential was ten times greater than hers, and she was raising his baby! WTF?

¡Ya ni modo! I don't know what his issues were, but I do know that we all have our demons. As I mentioned earlier, part of healing is learning to forgive. Forgiveness removes blinders and allows us to observe the good that results from experiences that aren't ideal.

Nana did just fine without him. Even throughout the Depression years, she provided for Wela, my mom, my aunt, and herself. Throughout her life, Nana managed to live, to support the upwardly mobile growth of loved ones, to Tythe, and to travel. She was not an educated woman, but she was the embodiment of integrity, discipline, faith, and a strong work ethic. Nana was the first female of color who was a superhero in my life.

It blows me away that my grandmother worked her fingers to the bone but never denied me a moment of play. It's something that I hold so dear to my heart because I meet women every day who won't allow themselves the gift of play. I've worked with successful, powerful women who have done amazing things, but ask them to open up their minds to some playtime, and they struggle.

Ironically, this lack of play has, for some, come with some severe consequences. At least two of my clients who struggled with letting loose to play suffered from debilitating illnesses. I'm not linking lack of play with sickness—I'm not a guru or a scientist—but from my observations, people who can't play tend to stress more.

These no-play types also tend to be people with high-stress jobs or responsibilities and significant control issues. I get it. I remember knowing how to play once, and then I remember losing it. It felt sudden, but it happened over several years. It was a subtle decline for me. I got bogged down with the business of life and simply lost my way. It can happen to anyone.

Somewhere in there we buy into all the things we think we should do, be, wear, and say, and we forget that we can honestly do, be, wear and say anything. I'm not saying go out and act a fool, but we can create a space to be free. It doesn't cost us a dime to play, and as a matter of fact, it can be the total opposite: We can make money from our playtime!

I love to play now. At particularly stressful times, I check myself in for some good playtime. I start playing with fantastic events, vacations, galas, screenings, and projects in my mind.

Play doesn't concern itself with the how of things; it just wholly indulges the thing itself. As a child, I didn't concern myself with how I would get the money for that plane ticket to the Bahamas. I didn't think about who I would have to meet to get invited to an elaborate party at a castle in France. I just focused on enjoying what it felt like to be there. I walked through those experiences in my mind, and the more I played, the more details I would add.

I didn't know that using my imagination would help me later in life when I studied Method acting. I loved acting because I could create a world that I may not ever have experienced in real life but that was exciting and felt alive. As an actress, I studied the techniques taught by the three American teachers associated with Method acting. Without getting nerdy and boring you to death, I'll just share with you a bit about each of the teachers and what I took from them.

Lee Strasberg is known as the father of Method. He focused on the psychological aspects of acting and used improvisation as well as affective memory. This technique requires actors to call on feelings prompted by being in a similar situation. Affective memory can be a challenge for people with limited experience. You'll sometimes hear of Method actors getting themselves in trouble because they take on a role too intensely.

People who have created psychological blockages to protect themselves emotionally also struggle with Method because they won't allow themselves to recall certain feelings easily. Back in the day, because of my blocks, I found it easier to tap into anger or rage. I found it more challenging to access emotional states that required vulnerability. Luckily for me, a brilliant woman also had an impact on my acting, and her name was Stella Adler.

If Lee Strasberg is the dad of Method, Stella Adler is certainly the mom. She preferred using imagination over just drawing on memories, and she emphasized the expression of thoughts and feelings through physical movement and behavior. She taught that if actors consistently examine the nuances of life, they can cultivate creativity and grow their toolbox! I didn't have to recall being a teenager in love; I could imagine it, watch it, and then be that. How exciting it was for me to become the embodiment of a character that had a different experience from my own. I could honor a role, not as imitation but as my version of that truth. Acting is not being fake; it's about being as real as you can get.

The third teacher was Sanford Meisner. He wasn't interested in memories at all. Instead, he wanted the actor to be intuitive and present, "to live truthfully under the imaginary circumstances." I also loved this addition to my arsenal because it helped me keep each scene fresh. With Meisner, the character is alive and in the moment. They're keenly aware of the subtle changes in the other actors' delivery of lines or body language. Meisner acting is much more reactive. While shooting *Mi Vida Loca*, I especially loved the scenes with the girls in the gang and on location in Echo Park—the way we walked together sometimes as one unit, always aware of the cars driving through the neighborhood. This hyper-awareness of space is something that I treasure even today.

## "LIVE OUT OF YOUR IMAGINATION, NOT YOUR HISTORY."

### – STEPHEN COVEY

Little did I know when I was studying these techniques as a young actress that I would use them later when I facilitated wellness workshops. These techniques had a value to me as an artist, but they aren't limited to those of us with an acting background, just like play isn't just a way to occupy kids. In the scientific community, these methods might be called visualization, visual motor rehearsal, or motor imagery.

Visualizing is the practice of talking yourself through— "seeing" yourself through—an event that has not yet taken place. Studies have demonstrated how effective these techniques can be for people of all walks of life.

For a more in-depth study on the subject, read *The Psychology of Winning* by Denis Waitley. Waitley used these techniques as a navy pilot in the 1950s, with NASA astronauts in the 1960s, and then in the 1980s as chairman of psychology on the US Olympic Committee's Sports Medicine Council.

In this chapter I explain how I learned to incorporate visualization techniques into my life and how all the experiences in my life suddenly began to make sense.

One of my coaches assigned a visualization exercise that would ultimately change my life. The task was simple: Just visualize myself on a day when I was living my best life. Superficially, an exercise like this might seem too simple to matter. I was a grown-ass woman hoping for career advancement, and this dude wanted me to do what? Daydream?

Luckily, I was open enough to try it.

At first, I was not good at it at all. It was like the kid I used to be had never existed. First I had to get over feeling like I was wasting time. Then I realized that even though I could intellectually understand what it meant to embark on a new journey, I was still full of fear. Every time I started to let myself explore, I would get caught up in HOW I was going to achieve my vision. Baby Gangsta wanted me to be realistic. So I decided to focus on the feeling of doing something I loved. In my mind, I began to create my "day in the life" clip. My first step was to not elaborate on it—it was just a simple bike ride with my kids through one of my favorite places in Los Angeles.

I wanted to create the clearest vision of this ride that I could. Here's the process I used: I closed my eyes and sat with my back straight and began to breathe deeply. I started to imagine the sights, the sounds, the smells, and even the taste of achieving what I wanted. As I went along, I allowed myself to feel the emotions that I would feel, as if this life were my reality.

**Visual:** I see my mint-green beach cruiser beneath me and my basket full of picnic supplies. I look back and see my kids behind me. We're on the road, headed to the beach. It's a weekday and there are only a few people around. The sun is out.

**Auditory:** I can hear the kids laughing and making fun of each other. As I pass by people, I catch snippets of various conversations on the streets. There are the occasional rings of other bikers' bells and the whisper of a slight breeze.

**Kinesthetic:** I feel the warm air on my body. As my bike moves down the street, this breeze almost tickles my skin. I notice a feeling of calm in my belly. I pay close attention and realize that it's the feeling of being free. I feel no tension; I have no place to rush to. I'm relaxed and connected to everything, even the bike and my surroundings. This is what being grateful feels like. I feel like smiling.

**Olfactory:** I smell the ocean, coffee from a small shop, and wood smoldering from bonfires the night before. I can also smell flowers from the gardens I pass. Finally, as we come to the boardwalk, the aroma of incense, food from vendors, and coconut from tanning oil are in the air.

**Gustatory:** I never really noticed, but there is a saltiness that lingers in the air by the beach.

The time I spent creating this scene in my mind was a blessing to me. Not only did I benefit from the time I spent in this meditation, but I can also honestly say that I manifested this life. On weekends I would ride to the beach on the mint-green cruiser a friend gifted me. I somehow found a way to spend time with my kids on weekdays. And the most important thing of all is that I began to feel the FREEDOM I so desperately craved.

See, this wasn't just about a bike ride. It was about the journey to feeling free. It all clicked for me when I understood that arriving at a desired feeling was a process. Since this time I have had the chance to live many times the reality I created first in my mind.

So what actually happened to me? How did I go from anxious to playful?

I allowed it! By observing the everyday beauty in my life, I was working on getting a grasp on what was pleasing to my senses. When I "came to my senses," a whole world was added to my actor's toolbox. I began adding more details to my imaginary life. Then I started taking the feelings from my imaginary world and mixing them into my real life.

I started acting again.

"Act as if" is a phrase and concept often recommended as a therapeutic technique for combating some forms of depression. The same practice is used in motivational sales training. "Acting as if" gives people the chance to create new scenarios in their minds first, then apply them to real life.

So how do we go from pretending to real life? For me, it broke down into two words: *communication* and *focus*.

First, let's talk about body language. How we use our body is a form of communication that's ever present but often ignored.

How do you picture someone sad or depressed? Hunched over, shallow breath, head down. Now visualize someone happy. Shoulders back, usually moving, head up, deep breath. Some scientists say body language accounts for between 55 and 90 percent of communication. Your brain will follow your body, and vice versa.

Free Angel had a way about her. She moved with confidence, she felt beautiful, healthy, and at ease. She took deep breaths and always seemed to smile. So, guess what I started to do more of? I put my shoulders back. I smiled more and took deeper breaths. I understood this because it was so very similar to Stella Adler's idea that the body can bring truth to a character that the mind doesn't yet know.

Now let's address our focus. We're in control of what our focus is on. When shit's hitting the fan, it can be hard to think about the things that make you happy. But this is precisely what you must train yourself to do! What would happen if you had a permanent HAPPY, high-resolution, full-color image in front of you ALL the time?

This is the power of visualization. If applied daily, it can quickly go from a picture in your mind to real life.

So focus and be sure of what you hope for. You're creating a roadmap to feeling good. Remember: You can use any picture to get there. You can replace the bike ride on the beach with your idea of heaven. I wanted freedom. You may wish for security, love, or confidence. If you want a house, make sure that you feel good in this house. You can create a cabin or mansion in your mind—it's all up to you. Just make sure that your feelings are aligned with what you really want.

You can achieve this by understanding what you value and what brings you joy. Don't hold back. Don't let feelings of lack prevent you from dreaming big or crazy. Just ask yourself, What do I want to see in my life, and how does it feel to have it?

At least five minutes of focusing on what you want is an essential part of making this work. You're focusing on how it feels when you do something that makes you happy. Society and the media make you think that happiness comes from outside influences. But I've come to believe that you have all you need inside you to manifest an incredible life. Does everything have to be perfect for you to experience this? NO! You're the creator of your own life.

Imagine the person you would be. How would you react to the great things happening? What would you say? Create that role. BE DESCRIPTIVE. Step into it. Take that person into your job, your family gatherings, your marriage. Try that role on for a week. If you don't like it, you can always go back.

Chances are that if you wear that super version of yourself, people won't recognize you. Some will want you to be that old version of yourself, and this is why you must practice. When creating the life you want, there will be challenges. Take those challenges into your visualizations and imagine yourself facing and overcoming them.

I want to share with you one of my experiences using creative visualization for manifestation. I was in the process of getting a divorce and losing my home. I didn't know how I was going to support myself or my kids in the costly city of Los Angeles. I had begun a daily meditation practice and was incorporating other forms of manifestation tools into my life. I had been using the visualization process as part of my meditation practice. This practice was almost like a mental workshop where I was building the life that I wanted to have. But it wasn't until a drive from Vegas to Los Angeles that I put these visions into my body.

The ride is pretty long, and whenever I left my sister's house in Nevada, I would leave at the crack of dawn to avoid traffic. The kids were asleep in the back that morning. I remember deciding not to turn on the radio. Instead, I indulged in an inner dialogue out loud. This was a conversation between me, myself, and I, and God. I remember feeling so good just being on that empty road while the sun came up. It reminded me of the times I would drive with my mom. We would spend hours talking about her life, and we'd write movie scripts that we thought should be made. On that drive from Vegas, I didn't miss my mom because I felt her in my spirit. I felt her presence and her love.

As the sun rose and created beautiful shifting patterns across the desert, I started speaking to the Angel in my visualizations. She was living my dream life. I began to recall the times when I was acting, and I would get scripts for parts that I was auditioning for. When I rehearsed I would use someone else's words, but I knew how to put myself in the moment completely. I could make it real for myself.

I started playing on this trip. I started delivering acceptance speeches to large audiences. And then I began to experience something profound. A prayer of gratitude for something that hadn't happened yet came across my lips. I began praying as a future Angel. I was thanking God for giving me more than I could have ever even dared to imagine and things that I couldn't have foreseen. I was humbled, I was grateful, and I was at the point of tears feeling such immense joy.

The trip seemed short and I felt almost high from the fantasy dialogue. The kids woke up and I was singing and happy. They were like, "What's up with Mom?" The people driving along the freeway were looking at me, and they must have thought I was crazy. And guess what? I didn't care! I decided that I didn't care who thought I was loony. When it came to joy, I was gonna get mine!

From that day forward, although I couldn't see proof, I continued to behave like my dreams and prayers had already come to pass. Shortly after that drive I got some news, and it was the delivery of an answered prayer. This answer was far beyond what I could have ever asked for or imagined.

One day, I was home packing boxes for a move that I was completely unsure of. My house was being sold and I needed to get out, but I didn't have a place to go. Everything in my world seemed to be going wrong. I had been doing contract work, but I now needed something stable. I kept putting out résumés but wasn't getting any responses. This kind of pressure would have ordinarily sent me into panic and deep depression. Yet, since that drive I'd been managing to keep the fear at bay. So I packed my things, making sure to take only what I really wanted in my life.

Then I got a call from a woman I casually knew from my son's school. She asked what we were doing for the summer. I'm a very private person, but something inside me just wanted to tell her the truth about my situation. I told her that I didn't know what we were doing for the summer and that quite frankly, I wasn't sure where I was even going to live. I had no job, my credit was garbage, and Los Angeles was EXPEN-SIVE. She listened quietly, then lovingly told me that it just so happened that she had a house that she wasn't living in and that she would love it if we moved in. The next day I went to pick up the keys to my beautiful home in Bel Air, California! A few weeks later, a former client called with a full-time job offer.

Now, you can choose to believe that this was the law of attraction, or God, or the power of visualization. Some of you may want to consider that this was just a coincidence. The specifics of your belief don't matter to me. What I'm trying to say here is that in my play, I allowed myself to be in the moment with every fiber of my being. When I spoke those words of gratitude from the future me, I delivered them with my tongue, my spirit, and my body. I had worked with a coach who told me about the importance of visualization. Still, it wasn't until that drive that I realized the actual power behind this tool. I felt the success and the joy—and the manifested vision became a part of every cell of my body.

So whether you call it "playtime," or "prayer time," "faith," or "imagination," this is a powerful mental, emotional, and spiritual tool.

So now I'm going to take YOU through the visualization process. Bear with me. If you're not used to it, you may feel awkward. That's okay. Keep at it. This is a POWERFUL technique. Find a quiet place if you can and reduce distractions as much as possible.

Let's go to the party.

If you're impaired in any way, you can modify this exercise and do it in your chair. If you can stand, please do so. If you can walk, I would like you to start walking in place. Take a deep breath. Close your eyes and look down toward your feet. I want you to take notice of the way your feet feel on the ground as you walk. With each step I want you to really use your imagination to transport your feet onto a path. This path is in your dream setting. It may be on a beach or in the mountains. Maybe you're at a relative's home or in the clouds. This is YOUR dream.

See that space under your feet. Notice the color, the texture, and the way your feet feel on the new surface. Take a breath and, keeping your eyes closed, begin to bring your eyes up. Start to take in the rest of the space. Look around you. Try to notice every detail. What time of day is it? Take a deep breath and inhale any aroma in the air. This is your dream spot, so it has to have a distinctive scent. Enjoy that smell. It gets more potent as you walk. Now, pay attention to how this place feels on your skin. Is it warm? Cool? It feels so good. Stretch your arms out and let your body enjoy this.

Now I want you to listen for something particular. Off in the distance you hear some music. Walk toward that sound. As you get closer, you recognize that it's your jam. It sounds so good. Go ahead and dance a bit. You LOVE this song. As you dance about, I want you to observe even more sounds. There's some laughter coming from a place that's very close by. You walk just around the corner and notice a sign that welcomes you as a guest of honor.

Right next to that sign is a mirror. When you look into it, you can see that you were transformed on this walk. You're dressed to the nines. You look so good! Go up to yourself and give yourself a high five. You've arrived!

Just beyond the mirror is a door. Go ahead and walk through that door. Walk into a celebration of you. As you walk into the center of this room, you notice around you all kinds of people. Maybe they're friends, perhaps they're people you've always wanted to meet. Some of you may have relatives who are no longer with us. For me, my mom is ALWAYS at my party. She always has a look of pride on her face. When you look at your guests, see the expressions on their faces. They're so happy to celebrate you. They're applauding your success and cheering you on. They know that you're already on the road to excellence, and they're proud.

Enjoy this time. If you want to, wave, throw kisses, and give hugs and high fives! It'll soon be time to go, but vow that you'll take this amazing feeling with you. Say it! "I'm taking all this with me! I'm taking joy. I'm taking peace, and I'm taking the celebration of me!"

It's time to say goodbye to your guests. You must start walking toward the exit door. Go through that door and come back to this reality. Come into this space, but know that you're different. In gratitude, say "THANK YOU." Take a deep breath. Stop walking in place. Let a smile come over your face. Feel the love and peace inside you. Open your eyes.

Welcome home.

# It's A Wrap

IN THE FIRST chapter, I mentioned that I facilitate wellness training workshops and coach people through complicated life transitions. For this book, it was suggested that I dive more deeply into my coaching practice, and I understand why. I have read countless books where people share examples of clients' problems and the solutions that evolved out of working together. I went back and forth on how I could share client success stories. I'm proud of the work that I do and prouder still of my amazing clients. Most of my clients are like me, equipped with a colorful past that tried to choke us out at one time. But somehow, we made it through and became ready to make the kinds of changes that transmute a lifetime of surviving into thriving. I have witnessed clients achieve levels of success in their relationships, at work, and in their businesses. And I have celebrated with my clients as they have learned to love, trust, and accept themselves and others more. But the truth is that the work I do with my clients is deeply personal, and I don't want to share specifics.

What I want to share is that I started my coaching as a client. As you have read, my life was falling apart around me, and I was desperate. Once my healing process had begun, and I no longer feared for my sanity, I began to want to find new ways to grow. That is where the coaching came in. There is a difference between coaching and therapy. The most significant difference is the focus of the work: therapy focuses on mental health and emotional healing, while life coaching focuses on setting and achieving goals. There is definitely a place for both. There are no games played in a good coaching relationship. A good coach will hold you accountable and expect you to want to make changes. When I hired my coaches, I was ready and willing to do the work. I was committed to creating and following a process that not only inspired me to achieve my goals but held me accountable. Accountability used to be a scary word for me. But as I've matured, and worked with some phenomenal people, I've realized it wasn't the accountability I had the problem with, it was the goal. I've learned that, if I don't do something that I set as a goal, there's no need for guilt, only a need for re-evaluation. I've found that if I'm connected to what I truly want, I find a way to go for it.

I started working as a life coach in 2011. I was not sure I wanted to be a life coach, per se. I had been coaching people on how to use social media for business, but it became clear that clients wanted something more. One of my first clients was an amazing, creative couple. I thought they were hiring me as a social media consultant, but they wanted me to help them improve their mindset. On our second call, one of them said, "When are we going to get to the other stuff? You know, the part about using our minds to make changes?"

I had been sharing my journey publicly for years. I didn't realize that people would pay to learn my process. At first, I didn't know what to charge, and I struggled to make a full-time living as a coach. Then, I committed to studying the abundance mindset and overcoming the limiting beliefs I had about money. I do a lot of work with others in the area of money mindset because many of us struggle in our relationship with money. For those who don't know, the statistics regarding Latinas and the wage gap are dismal. I am not saying that attitudes about money are the only reason we are paid less. Obviously, discrimination and bias play their part. Still, I think self-awareness, financial literacy, and the courage to grow are critical to our ability to build wealth and sustain our communities.

In 2015, after a call from my friend Jesse Borrego, I decided it was time to put my release from anxiety to the test. For years I had been invited to go appear at car shows or special events, but honestly, I wasn't sure if I could handle being in a crowd. From 2011, I had diligently worked on managing my anxiety. I had conquered my fear of planes, elevators, and cars. It was time to step even further outside my comfort zone. Jesse convinced me to have a conversation with an incredible shop owner in Houston. After one chat with Margarita, I found myself on my way to sign autographs for hundreds of people. I did not have the heart palpitations I feared I might feel when spotting the long line that led to her stall at the International Flea Market. Anxiety was replaced with a feeling of complete love and liberation. People waited on line for six hours to chat, hug, share their stories, and take pictures. I realized that every moment of my life had occurred so that I could be in that spot.

I want to share with you that this was not about me being famous because truthfully, it is Sad Girl who is the icon. It's Sad Girl who has won the hearts of so many people. I just showed up with her face and gave out the love, empathy, and compassion that I had grown into as Angel. And as I listened to the stories shared, and histories told, it became evident that I had been given a gift that I had to share on a broader scale than I ever knew.

When we started Living Firme, my partner Cynthia Carranza (Sparkles) and I knew we wanted to impact the community in more ways than one. I had been blessed to play Sad Girl and wanted to find a way to help as many businesses thrive as possible. Our business model started out as a crazy smörgåsbord of offerings. We sold gear, produced cultural events, hosted business networking events, and booked speaking engagements. But all along, what I really wanted to do was facilitate abundance mindset and wellness seminars. And I wanted to have our workshops in neighborhoods that most big-name speakers would probably never think to visit.

Our first seminar happened in a little shop owned by a friend in Highland Park. The sold-out event was life-altering for so many people. News of that seminar spread like wildfire. Before we knew it, we were asked to do workshops all over the place and for organizations that I never thought I'd be invited into. Soon we started to run virtual mastermind groups for people who could not make it to our live events. While growing our business, we've made a ton of mistakes. We love sharing our mistakes with our business Mastermind members because those are the lessons we paid for. Sharing is how we help others grow.

I became a transformative coach, wellness trainer, and speaker because of the fires I've walked through. I've learned that anxiety was never my enemy it was just my emotional barometer. The barometer is not the source of rain it's merely the machine that measures atmospheric pressure. The world offers up all sorts of things that add to pressure, but now I know how to read the device.

I pay close attention to my inner dialogue and my outer world. Over the years, I've become super hip to triggers. I still fall for them sometimes, but I no longer use perfection as a metric for my success. Instead, I celebrate the victories, the growth, and even my ability to cope.

Now, I want to express as much love and feel as much joy as I possibly can from every day. I maintain a constant relationship with God. I recognize that no matter how spiritual I get, I will always be just a little loca.

And that's okay with me.

I love my life because I love the version of me living it. But make no mistake, life still presents its challenges. There are so many stories and people I didn't get to share about in these pages. For example, I didn't get into too many details about my kids. My kids are such an enormous part of my life, but I kept them out of this book because they are young and still developing. They deserve the right to have some privacy while they navigate their individual journeys.

Another part of my current situation that I skipped, on purpose, is my love life. My partner is the wind beneath my wings. For the first few years of our courtship, I kept him all to myself. He would come to events, but only my closest friends would know who he was. One day, I plan to co-author a book that chronicles our special kind of love. I will cover how we met, how we grew together, and how we keep our relationship spicy.

I'm still learning, and life continues to be an incredible ride.

I'm grateful that you chose to come this far with me, and I'm so excited for you to continue finding ways to pump up the volume on your peace and happiness. There's a whole world inside you waiting to be further explored and discovered, but it doesn't end at you.

How do you now take what you've learned and become a powerhouse of service in your community? In the hundreds of meetings and events I've attended, I've learned that there's an endless supply of people in need. Some folks will benefit from your newly acquired interest in mindfulness, conscious eating, and commitment to moving qi. ¿Y sabes que? (You know what?) You don't have to be a guru to share.

You may have picked up this book thinking it would chronicle the life of a Los Angeles gang banger. Who knows—maybe you just liked the cover, featuring Sad Girl by chingona artist Denise Cortes! But if you're still here, no matter where you come from, you're transforming. You've lived every moment of your life for a reason. You've been a survivor.

Now be a thriver and share your magic.

And speaking of sharing, if you liked this book, I would really appreciate it if you'd share it with the people you know. Authoring is an entirely new hustle for me. Your ratings and reviews help newbies like me get noticed in the literary world. Everyone has a story, and I'd like to see even more diversity in the self-help section.

Be kind to yourself. Positivity, empathy, love, and compassion are learned skills. Skills are the expertise or talent needed in order to do a task. Your task is to live your best life every damn day. If you can wear a smile that comes from within your soul and is infectious, you win!

As you grow, do your best to bless people and circumstances, then let them go. You won't always do or say the right thing. Be humble, but don't stop looking for the authentic voice. Keep growing.

I hope to see you all soon. Maybe we'll meet at some of the live events I do through my company Living Firme. Maybe we'll chat online. You can always find me online at TooHappyToBeSadGirl.com

Whether our paths cross or not, I'm sending you the very best of intentions for the next stage of your life.

Al rato.

# About the Author

*A*NGEL AVILES LIVES her life purpose as, a national speaker, transformational coach, dynamic workshop facilitator, business owner, content producer, mom, volunteer, food justice advocate, tech evangelist, passionate Latina, soulmate, seeker, traveler, former actress, and most of all, genuinely human.

# Acknowledgments

To my tribe:

So many of you have touched my life in so many ways. Thank you all.

To my kids:

For me you are ALL the sun, the moon, and the stars. I really had no idea that I could open up to a love this big until I met each of you. You ALL fill me with hope. You ALL have made me laugh and cry. If I had to do it again, I would choose a life with each and every one of you, exactly as you are. You have been my most inspiring teachers.

To my fam:

Many members of my family are mentioned in this book, but I don't talk enough about how special my family is. We are a small group but we love each other. I am who I am in spite of and because of you all.

To my king:

A special thanks to the man who insisted I come to know my worth. I fought you tooth and nail, but you urged me to step into the gap and be what I said I wanted to be. You push me to keep growing. If I'm honest, hate the levels of discomfort you challenge me to, but I love YOU to the moon.

To my besties:

I have so many acquaintances but just a few people who are my true ride-or-die folks. Y'all know who you are. You've known me at my best and worst, and you've stuck by me. You've blessed me and I'm so grateful.

Made in the USA
Middletown, DE
25 August 2024